CYBERPUNK
CONSPIRACY
MIND OVER MATTER

FURTHER CONSPIRACIES?!

If you would like to read further on the New Age Conspiracy to elevate Human Consciousness on this Planet and elsewhere—don't simply ask your book dealer to order the following titles—**Demand that S/He do so!** They are:

THE FUTURE HISTORY SERIES
By Timothy Leary, Ph.D.

Info-Psychology
Neuropolitics
The Intelligence Agents
What Does Woman Want?
Millenium Madness
The Game Of Life

THE ROBERT ANTON WILSON SERIES

The Cosmic Trigger
Sex and Drugs
Coincidance: A Head Test
Wilhelm Reich In Hell
Prometheus Rising
The Goddess Obsession
The New Inquisition

THE FUTURE IS **NOW** SERIES

UNDOING YOURSELF with Energized Meditation and Other Devices
  By Christopher S. Hyatt, Ph.D. Introduced by Israel Regardie,
  With an extensive Foreword by Robert Anton Wilson.
UNDOING YOURSELF TOO by Christopher S. Hyatt, Ph.D.
Breaking The GodSpell: Genetic Evolution By Neil Freer.
  Introduced by Zecharia Sitchin.
The Sapiens System—The Illuminati Conspiracy: Their Objectives, Methods & Who They Are!
  By Donald Holmes, M.D.
  With an extensive introduction by Robert Anton Wilson.
Angel Tech — A Modern Shaman's Guide to Reality Selection by Antero Alli,
  Preface by Robert Anton Wilson.
All Rites Reversed! by Antero Alli
The Akashic Record Player by Antero Alli
An Interview with Israel Regardie — His Final Thoughts
  Edited by Christopher S. Hyatt.
Zen Without Zen Masters By Camden Benares.
Monsters and Magical Sticks: There Is No Such Thing As Hypnosis?
  By Steven Heller, Ph.D. Introduced by Robert Anton Wilson.
The Shaman Warrior By Gini Graham Scott, Ph.D.

For a free catalog of all Falcon titles write to:
FALCON PRESS □ 3660 N. 3rd. St. □ Phoenix, AZ 85012 □ U.S.A.

CYBERNETIC CONSPIRACY

MIND OVER MATTER

By Constantin Negoita, Ph.D.

1988
Falcon Press
Phoenix, Arizona 85012 U.S.A.

ISBN: 0-941404-69-2
Library of Congress Card Catalog Number: 88-80257

First Edition — 1988

Cover Design and Art Work: D'vorah Curtis
Typesetting Design: Cate Mugasis

Falcon Press
3660 N. 3rd St.
Phoenix, Arizona 85012
(602) 246-3546

Manufactured in the United States of America

conspiratio = a breathing together (magna amoris conspiratione consentientis tenuit amicorum greges, Cicero: de Finibus Bonorum et Malorum, 1.65)

spiritus = breathing (poetam quasi divino quoddam spiritu inflari, Cicero: pro Archia, 18)

★

Like all big universities, ours was involved in advanced research. Like all scientists, we had been advised to apply for a grant. That winter we were supposed to meet a deadline and write a proposal to the Science Foundation. The proposal was supposed to be intelligible enough for a scientifically literate reader.

Filled with concern, we examined this vague requirement. There was some cause for concern, but no need for alarm. The reader should understand everything by getting a glimpse of only one topic sentence stating the thesis. This sentence should include the primary objectives, the scope of the project, the technique and the approaches. We had the technique and the approaches, but we were still hesitating about the primary objectives and the scope.

All our effort was concentrated towards writing that sentence. Definitely, the quality of the proposal was critically dependent upon its wealth, precision, and beauty.

The proposal was vital for our promotion because we were the last comers in the new department of Information Science, and the department was striving to get visibility.

Our field was Approximate Reasoning. In those days, many authoritative colleagues were sure that though the differences between biological and artificial intelligence are of course enormous,

3

they are not of kind but of degree. We examined this enormous assumption and decided to avoid it, even if at risk.

We knew that tradition: that handing down of opinions and customs, could kill discovery and invention. We knew that our peers, always jealous if you don't quote them at length, always keep you in their shadow. We tried to avoid the traps and the sneers. Some of our snivelling colleagues were proof that a promise could be a delusion. We fought our way.

First, we had a suspicion that the differences between men and machines are not of degree but of kind. Then we noticed that man can handle vague concepts. The study of vagueness was only a philosophical hobby for one's leisure time, like growing blue roses. We decided to focus our attention on this forgotten subject.

Then, we settled on a heated and sometimes emotional flurry of talks in which we surveyed the last journals and the last books. When a paper appears in a scholarly journal it is widely viewed with respect. After all, it comes with what might be called the good seal of approval; it has passed the muster of peer review.

We spent hours between the shelves. We almost moved into the library. But the pace was too severe to be kept up for long. With pitying smiles, silent reproaches and shocked responses, we moved to the reference room, where the goddess of joy, supported by long powerful legs, made our hearts stop. Our conclusion was that she was the symbol of symmetry. Her hemispherical breasts were violent documents in proof of his claim. Her legs displayed that this was the truth.

We questioned this truth and speculated about its degrees. D.R. of the Apes supposed evolutionary reasons why women evolved hemispherical breasts, like buttocks. John rejected his vulgarities with the argument that women are biologically superior. Believe me, they have instinct, while the man usually has only pride.

We did not always understand D.R. He and his wife had separated early. There was an attempt at reconciliation, but it ended in the midsts of an earthquake. He had shut the door behind him and stood beating his bare hands against his shanks. He knows what he has lost in those days after he has lost the doe. He had matured, as his culture counted maturing. But he had broken something older than ancient. The tender heart. The saintliness. Losses worth the weeping . . . now he was hungry for power, and fighting with John.

John was intelligent enough to have patience, to smile to everybody and do nothing in haste. He had once had this experience. Then he served three years in the senate, after which the provost had said, "Thank you John, now you are free to go into full research," and he was happy to start a new life with new people.

He was the one to say that the basic thing, in order to send a proposal, was to adopt a basic assumption. He was the one to suggest a regular meeting; an emotional flurry of talks, where we discussed the last books, and discussed the last ideas. He suggested D.R. to take his place in the senate.

At its one hundred and sixty-sixth meeting, the senate approved him, and the provost said, "Thank you D.R., I am sure that you will play an important role in the college, that you will help me in my responsibilities as a provost, and that you will help your colleagues with their proposal," D.R. blushed, thanked, promised, and perspired.

Then, we wrote a short paper, sent it to be published, and D.R. was the reviewer. We didn't know why but his review was awful, terrible, dreadful.

We invited some people for a short conference of two days in which he was amazingly aggressive, leering at our conclusions.

Only John said that he would recover, he did so before. I remember what happened when D.R. was hurt by the goddess from the reference room, and said that there are limits for everything, and the girl laughed louder and louder, and her hips waggled when she laughed in convulsions.

We continued to invite him to our meetings, which continued to be flurries of emotional talks about the last books, and the last ideas, and the last gossip.

Of course, there were pitying smiles, silent reproaches, numerous questions, and shocked responses; but this is life on the campus.

When we were blessing the university womanhood: the trim, the taunt, and the wholly tones; and when we were making comments about smooth, firm shaped legs, he always supposed evolutionary reasons why women evolved hemispherical breasts as symbols.

Someone noticed that there is a current and exceedingly stupid doctrine that symbol evokes emotion and exact prose states reality. D.R. was always against it, feeling that nothing could be more stupid and more further from the truth. Exact prose abstracts from reality and symbol presents it. For that very reason, symbols have some of the many-sidedness of wild nature. And for hours we analyzed what is subjective and what is objective in the vision of the prophet Isaiah, in which he saw God seated on a throne, high and lifted up; in a house filled with glory and surrounded by seraphims, each with six wings: two to cover the face, two to cover the feet, and two for flying.

All this happened before the one hundred and ninety-sixth meeting of the University Senate which was convened in room two-zero-four, where D.R. presented a report and thanked the university for the opportunity to have served for six years. He was then looking for a full-time teaching and research post. The provost thanked him on behalf of the senate for the work he had done, and said that he always admired the commitment which D.R. had brought to the office and to the students. "I can tell you that everything D.R. says he really means," he said, "because I have gotten to know him in working closely with him in my responsibilities as a provost, and they were interesting encounters. Believe me, we should all be grateful for that. Thank you D.R. Now you are going into full-time research and teaching, and will continue to play an important role in the college, deeply related with what the university is fundamentally about: academic quality and academic excellence."

D.R. accepted the invitation to serve as a member in the Council of Honors, blushed, thanked, promised, perspired, and finally declared his interest in doing some research. The provost suggested our team, which badly needed some help for writing a report to be sent to the Science Foundation, which, thank God, always gives us the money. The goal was to speed our writing because D.R. was an excellent manager, being able to build and follow a schedule.

We did not like the idea.

We reacted first with a verse from Cavafi. "As you set out for Ithaca, hope your road is a long one, full of adventure, full of discovery. Keep Ithaca always in your mind. Arriving there is what you are destined for, but do not hurry the journey at all, better it will last for years."

D.R. did not like the idea.

Then we quoted Corinthians and told him that brothers, when they meet together, everyone with a hymn to sing, or a word of instruction, or a doctrine to impart, or an interpretation, or ready to speak in strange tongues, should see that all is done to their advantage.

Skeptical, D.R. declared that there can be little doubt that these advices are good, but the way in which they can be applied in our case is less clear and therefore, the first step in the clarification process must be the adoption of a basic assumption. We needed practical results. We had to avoid being misunderstood by those who would judge our research, who could kill us for spending their physical money on useless, elusive, metaphysical constructs.

We answered him, "No, don't be afraid of Cyclops, angry Poseidon, you will never find things like that on your way, as long as a rare excitement stirs our spirit."

So we sketched out the backbone of our delayed report and the text sounded vague, like a creed. We wrote that we explored a conceptual framework needed to explore the process we call qualitative change. Our conclusion was that all contradictions are reconciled in higher synthesis. Another conclusion was that if we explore the procedure of building overlapping descriptions, and the way in which natural language is involved in this process, then getting a feel for the whole is nothing else than transcendence; a constant openness through which man grasps freedom. The last idea was simple. We declared that it was high time to obtain a deep insight into this natural process; that we needed more time and more money.

Our decision was to work hard to develop these ideas, because genius is only one percent inspiration and all the rest is plain effort. We did not want to repeat a series of other attempts, when we did not pay too much attention to our seemingly inability to finish what we had started. Therefore, we decided to meet almost every evening, secretly, in the oldest wing of the campus, now almost deserted.

We liked a room in the old department of physics, where the blackboard wasn't black any more. There, uncountable white stripes, cracks filled with white chalk, witnessed uncountable lectures delivered by proud teachers ready to swear that all the secrets of nature were already known. We started to joke about these poor teachers who believed in the meter engraved on a platinum bar between two fine scratch marks, and later, in the wavelength of light, geared not to everyday life on earth, but to the abstruse dictates of Einstein's relativity physics.

This was a historical room where once the enlightened opinion ridiculed the idea that something is coming from nothing, with the argument of conservation laws which proudly state that certain things are immortal. The list of quantities thought to be strictly conserved included energy, electrical charge, and the baryon number, and we imagined how thousands of students were fooled by the sound of the words and the mystique that surrounds them.

Of course, when everybody understood the eternal power of matter, the department of physics received a new building and funds for more research. Only then the students found out about beautiful grand unified theories, leading to the simple conclusion that there is no law that prevents evolving out from nothing.

We chose the old room because it was close to the library, a donation as a memorial to those patrons of rational thinking who wanted to strike a valiant blow against all mystical thinking. There, in that huge library, nobody listened to our snickers, titters, and guffaws when we discovered how Petrus Sabatius Justinian shut down the Academy of Plato in the tenth century of its full operation. Like a stone was Petrus Sabatius, like a super stone, smashing the Academy on its feet. Then the whole of it broke into small pieces, and was actually blown away by the wind. John Philiponus opened the imperial eyes. He spoke against the Aristotelian notion that the stars must be the eternal rotors of the eternal motion we call the natural process. He observed that some stars seem to shine with different colors than others. Arguing by analogy with terrestrial fires, which glow in different colors when different substances are thrown into them, he reasoned that some process must be going on there. If so, that process must have a beginning, an end, and a life, contrary to Aristotle's view of the everlastingness of celestial motion.

And we laughed for hours, sure that laughter has to do with logic, because it is possible to trace everything laughable to a syllogism with two premises, one undisputed and one unexpected.

We used to spend hours between the library shelves, and other hours in the reference room, where we chatted with the same blonde with the full sensuous mouth, long-lashed blue eyes, opulent breast, and a serious concern about dreams, particularly those dreamt by a noted scholar called Daniel, who left a memorial after death to the common benefit of mankind concerning things at the end of the world.

With her stark earthbound personality, with the stare of her eyes and an elegance based on symmetry—perfect symmetry—she was a prophetess carrying the burden of truth. There was something behind this symmetry, and if one couldn't say exactly what it was, it seemed to have to do with muted despair and mourning for a beautiful world in which not man but God was inevitable to seed.

She was beautiful and we were sensitive to her beauty. She had a beautiful smile ready to blow into hard laughter whenever the premises of our syllogisms were one undisputed, and one unexpected. This was a sure sign that she liked logic, the main item in the arsenal of our secular weapons.

At the beginning, we considered Daniel's book as a poem. Our theory was that art can be encountered only by direct experience. We read and reread great poems generation after generation. We mount new interpretations of the great plays. We keep the great instrumental works alive in the repertoires of orchestras, but we don't perform a discovery again and again. On the contrary, we re-perform a scientific work only when its greatness comes into question.

She did not agree. She was convinced that science mounts new interpretations of the old secrets. And she tried to convince us to examine the facts.

At the beginning we hesitated. Our silence was a kind of fear of error. And of ridicule. Observant, vigilant, watchful, we were on the look-out for danger, as in our current attempt to question the wisdom of the blessed Aristotle, because with all due respect we seriously questioned his wisdom.

Of course, we were scared. It seems ironic that a scientist whose job is to observe and report without the fetters that governe the everyday discourse, should be unwilling to follow his instincts. But this was a natural reflex considering the power of the tradition. As scientists we were entrusted with the responsibility of accurate reporting. Any stupid error was going to hurt our career, depending on our sound judgement. Believe me, there is no fear stronger than that of losing your job when your career is a calling. A career is one part duty, one part fear, and one part ambition, but a calling is four parts awe.

In our room in the old wing of the campus where the blackboard seemed to be useless, we decided to polish our ideas, get rid of the fear, and finish the report. Undisturbed by indiscrete lay ears, we wanted to avoid the mocking of others as had happened before at a congress where somebody very important asked if we were going to change the tradition of two values in logic: the indubitable true-false-and-nothing-else-in-between.

We tried to explain to the blonde, and she seemed to follow that the simple yes-no used to answer crisp questions without equivocation, without any doubt or any suspicion that in between could exist shades, does not match the vagueness of our natural language. She seemed to follow easily.

We went a step further. We tried to explain to her why the mathematical world was astounded by the proof that any given collection of initial statements leads to a system of propositions that can be neither proved nor disproved to be true. Worse still, we said, there are propositions that can be both disproved and proved. So she found out with amazement that as if it were not bad enough to live in an undecidable world, for some propositions we cannot even decide if they can be decided, or in some cases, whether the decidability is decidable, and so on in an infinite chain.

The blonde seemed to be fascinated by our purr. On any given phrase which we produced slowly, we sounded mesmerizing. We approached each phrase in the same breathy swooning croon. After listening to consecutive ideas with the same vocal tone, she seemed to ache to hear us cut loose. Our compositions effectively presented fundamental scientific discoveries, most of them being slight; just ten words, elegantly phrased and rephrased.

When she asked us what is mathematics, we told her about the uncountability of the set of all numbers. There are more real numbers than natural numbers; there are weak, strong, huge, exorbitant, supercompact, inaccessible, measurable, indescribable and extendible cardinal numbers, and despite the variety of their names, experienced mathematicians can order them according to size, and even announce which ones exist, which ones probably do exist, which ones might exist, and so on.

Here, she started to laugh with all her face, and so we did. Then she started to laugh with all her body, and so we did. Of course, we postponed any conclusion, any misleading conclusion that can be later regretted.

Once somebody came up with the bold observation that although in natural language infinite is a negative word, meaning not finite, in mathematics infinity is defined in positive terms when something exists and the finiteness is restrictive, or negative. Her laughter was convulsive, and we all joined in the laugh.

Once, we came up with the fact that the classics defined an infinite set as being linked one-to-one with a proper subset, which means that the whole is included in parts. The spasm of mad laughter didn't end for a long time.

So we stayed friends.

Scientists are strange. Their personal visions of the world inform their work and present it in a unique way. They are able to see, in even familiar situations, things one hadn't noticed or fully comprehended previously. Therefore, uncharted expanses of the universe, or the secret world within, are revealed with sometimes painful clarity. This is what we said.

Without any premeditation or secret intention, she told us about her new paintings. We were pleased.

The first one was a masterful rendition of nature, which she called spring, Sunday afternoon. "The Real," she said, and we all smiled.

The second was a white canvas. "The Super-Real," she said. The artist admits it is a challenge. It is not the super rich figured piece which is a blank tablet, but the mind of the viewer when he first confronts it. We must bring our interpretation to this work approaching it with the clean slate of an open mind. Our laughter began to be convulsive.

Another one was an outer canvas painted solid with white acrylic, framed images set some inches behind it. The inset forms were three-dimensional. Some were hung before the matting. One employed scraps of canvas painted with oil stick. The figures beared no relation with the outside world. A dead white structure. The spasm of our long laughter didn't end for a long time. "The Surreal," she said, and joined in crisp laughter.

So we stayed friends.

Artists are strange. Their personal vision of the world presents their work in a unique way. Through art we can see a secret world beyond the surface of life. This is what she said.

★

No one witnessed our endless discussions in the old department of physics, but there was no one who did not know that something was going to happen; that something was going to be discovered, according to the booklet from the Science Foundation which says that discovery is the product of opportunity, imagination, brilliance, persistence and serendipity. An enlightened society must recognize the major opportunities in unfettered research in which imaginative scientists feel free to pursue their curiosity beyond the limits of available knowledge.

Going beyond the surface was the idea, the main idea, the tremendous idea, and we were full of new ideas. Better said, of new concepts, or better still, of very old concepts buried from a long time, almost dead, since the sagacious mind of the Aristotelians explored the deepest questions of metaphysics and embraced eighteen arguments against creation. Their idea was that beyond the surface there is nothing. We were challenging their challenge. That was what we told the girl, half-joking, and she seemed to follow with interest.

In fact, our job was to try a theory of vagueness. Our first step had been to explore the structure of concepts. In the library we confessed to the blonde goddess what we had discovered. She seemed to follow.

We told her how these marvelous concepts, although different, are overlapping. We told her also that these concepts have the power of combination, like individuals who are subject to sexual reproduction. By synthesis, the concepts go up to abstractions. She didn't have any difficulty following. Encouraged, we ventured a little bit further.

The big laughter with opulent breasts volunteered to give us a hand. She looked in the special collections, determined to find proof that the first nonaristotelians had the same intentions. One day she came up with a text written by Leontius from Byzantium, a friend of Petrus Sabatius and John Philiponus. We were amazed how easy she found it.

This guy, in the sixth century, observed that our impressions are vague, not revealing the truth, and if we attempt a division into genera, the overall view is lost; we are heading not towards the truth, but toward an infinite regress.

Then the laughing, twinkling eyes of the blonde struck our laughter-loving brains, and the laughing-bird started to laugh with a combination of spasmodic utterance of inarticulate sounds, facial distortion, shaking of the sides, and swaying of the hips; oh, the graceful swaying of hips.

Our prompt reply was visible, vocalized laughter, more than a simple expression of mirth. We understood that man has a faculty of the ludicrous in his mental organization, and muscles in his face make possible this expression.

She was so generously open to intellectual chat, so happy to discover the mystic vibration of the soul when one can read the heart of the other, that she sometimes failed to realize how much she was being used as an indicator or measure of our own feelings and thoughts. For the marvelous thing about her was not the way in which she deliberately introduced critique or applaud into her laugh, though as time went on, with encouragement from us, she did do more and more of this; but the way in which she never held back her sharp, explosive, barking-like exhalations, if they were relevant to the subject.

Even when she had doubts and held up her finger reprovingly, her laughing eyes belied the gesture. Once, when we said that Aristotle defined the ridiculous as that which is incongruous but does not represent pain or danger, she burst out laughing as if this was the most unheard of thing she had ever heard of.

We believed for a while that her pleasure of laughter grew from a sense of our misfortune and a sudden awareness of superiority in that she was not in the predicament observed. Then the means by which she worked her magic was by using laughter as a form of approval.

This was the reason that we did not understand how to take her silence. We all said that something had to be there, when she did not laugh; something worth being discovered, according to the booklet from the Science Foundation which says that discovery is the product of opportunity and persistence.

In the days when our friendship had become closer than before, when we discussed at length inaccessible, exorbitant, indescribable numbers and about the infinite chain of the parts including the whole; she laughed like a bell. Then John Philiponus tried to pinpoint the mistake made by many philosophers of science who do not see how to stop the infinite chain. His presentation was short.

In the period of the fathers, he said, the relation between the Son and the Spirit was disputed. The idea was that the Spirit comes from the Father shining forth through the Son. After the ninth century, the West reproached the East that they did not admit the Son as a source. Patriarch Gregory made a distinction between the eternal shining forth of the Spirit and his coming into existence. This coming forth of the light coincides with the ray from which the light receives neither existence nor being, but only comes to perception. His main conclusion was that shining forth means coming to rest. Rest can be explained as an end to all further departing, as an abiding, a lasting. This procession towards the Son, in whom he comes to remain, means that the origin is only the Father; for otherwise this would mean that the Spirit goes forth from the Son, instead of coming to rest into him, and the Godhead would be capable of an infinite unwinding. An endless multiplication of the divinity is avoided and an internal unity is achieved.

The girl did not laugh.

We were all born of different religions and most of us were not practicing any, so it was rather difficult to know in what church she could have been baptized.

Once we said to her with violence, tell us why you did not laugh, but she did not answer us. Later, when D.R. tried to enter our discussions, we did not know what was said but we did know that one time the blonde said to him, "you have no right to ask any question," and he said, "why not?" "You will never realize their thinking," she said, laughing.

Our position was not only unique within the university at that time, but was probably unprecedented in the whole history of the subject. This is not to say, of course, that all our colleagues or even the majority of them have accepted our ideas. They have not. After all, the nonaristotelian logic was a rather esoteric subject which few people had even heard of, and fewer still knew anything about until very recently.

Those who were not familiar with our work were wondering what possible connection there might be between a field of study as specialized as nonaristotelian logic and the better known and obviously important field of computers. This was the question we wanted to answer in our report to the Science Foundation. We tried a rehearsal in the reference room.

We explained to the goddess that it has often been suggested that man is most clearly distinguished by the faculty of intelligence and she agreed. We defined intelligence by conceptualization. She did not say anything. It was only natural to ask what contribution the study of conceptualization can make to our understanding of intelligent behaviour, but she still did not say anything. We continued with a little bit more jargon.

We developed a model of concepts in order to give a mathematical definition to some of the most striking features of these concepts. Of particular importance in this connection is the ability that humans have to capture more and more reality by moving towards more and more abstraction. The most abstract concept of something seems to be a terminal object in a very fine structure, governed by very fine laws, described by a very fine language, just invented by very fine mathematicians.

She seemed to be puzzled.

We tried to give an example. Those who did not escape the influence of scholasticism of the last few centuries, we said, claimed that they can fully grasp the reality by means of reason. They run the risk of soon having to replace the explanation of today with others, for today's explanations will soon prove insufficient for the minds of tomorrow. Science does not make earlier formulations obsolete when it pulls back to new ones. It remains in continuity with them. But the final view has to be one of maximum vagueness.

This was a liberating solution. She burst out in laughing like never before, and her shaking of the sides was more convincing than ever; her sharp, explosive exhalations convinced us that this was the most unheard of thing she had ever heard of. We were sure that her laughter grew out of a sense of the misfortune of mankind which will never be able to have a general view of the world.

Patiently we tried to explain the mechanism of the view. "Take your dog," we said. "He is one from the set of all dogs. You cannot give a name to all the existing and coming dogs in the world. Therefore you are using a label and this is the word dog."

With sheer, gleeful laughter she answered that she only had a cat, and we understood that she understood and continued in the same breathy swooning croon. It was perfectly clear that after listening to consecutive arguments with the same vocal tone, she did not ache to hear the singers. So we went further.

Now consider all the dogs and cats was the next song. You can cover these two sets with a new label, say pets, and so on and so on, until you reach the top of them which is the famous vague label "something."

The laughing-bird held up the finger reprovingly. Her laughing eyes belied the gesture, and we laughed like a bell. This time our laughter was a form of approval and our conclusion was that she was the goddess of beauty.

So by our persuasion the blonde was introduced to the private lessons of nonaristotelian logic. She yielded to the voice of reason and enthusiasm. She accepted the new creed according to which good and bad can be simultaneously true.

We warned her that this new faith would be rewarded with suspicion, skepticism, and loss of support from the most respectable people. No answer was returned, until the silence of astonishment, doubt and contempt was broken by laughter. Then we persevered in the exercise of our mission.

Soon, people hardened in their unbelief by superstition, and envy colored their malice with the pretence of established traditions. As the terms of communion were insensibly narrowed, and the authority of the classical logic was exercised with increasing severity, we were called upon to renounce and to bury the standard of rebellion. We heard laments about the magnitude of the evil. The superstition had not only infected our department but had even spread itself into the library, into the reference room. Our predictions of the failure of knowledge inspired the establishment with the apprehension of some danger which would arise from the new message. An implacable and unrelenting zeal filled many breasts against us. Whatever our skeptical view was, our inflexible obstinacy appeared deserving of punishment. Armed with captious syllogisms from the logic of Aristotle, the subtle D.R. was an invincible disputant, whom it was impossible either to silence or to convince. Such talents engaged our friendship. This strategy proved to be fruitful. Our weapon was our laughter.

From the beginning we detected hesitation, ambivalence, and, especially, fakery in his smile. If there is one human display that qualifies as a fixed pattern, it is the tendency of people in certain situations to draw back the corners of their mouths and expose their teeth. The play of the risorius, the facial muscle that governs the smile and made D.R. risible, spelt the difference between peaceful coexistence and romance.

D.R. was of the opinion that unrestrained laughter is not characteristic of the wise and strong. He either smiled or barked.

We thought the surest sign of a healthy spirit is to see friendly joyfulness pour all over the features, down into the throat and the muscles of the body without bound or hindrance. But we have clearly distinguished laughter from the curling of the lip in scorn. The temper of these two acts is opposite and their neural machinery distinct, as might be seen in the fact that the girl laughed with both sides of the face, but D.R. sneered only with one.

The girl was always starting with a flash, because the motion of the upper lip came first, and so strongly, that it used to broaden a little as it rose, so that while all the teeth shone, the mouth was redder than it was: the cheeks curved and the eyes gathered light, attracting the brows and lashes toward them, warming their vivid glitter with radiant soft lines.

D.R. was different. His jeer, gibe, leer, scoff, flout, hoot, gird, niggle, taunt, and the lash of sarcasm were all cold. He gibed at all our mathematical proofs, and we endured his taunts as heros do. His jeering remarks were rude. He was always leering, and at the beginning he tried to make us the scoff of the campus. But he never said anything about the girl, or anything she said, even later when she gave us an intimate and engaging account of her formative years.

She told us once about the spiritual pilgrimage of her generation, the detachment from the ideals of the forebears: from the myth of infinite progress, from the faith in the decisive role of science to establish peace and social justice, from the landscape of the twentieth century covered with fallen and blind believers in progress and with their victims. We understood that she was able to understand the idea of an infinite regress.

She told us also that for some of her generation, positive thinking and a serious study of the prophets could constitute a new age movement. She quoted at length from a book written by Eliade, a Sewell Avery Distinguished Service Professor of the History of Religion at the University of Chicago, who said that we are not just biological cousins of the aboriginals, but friends and collaborators in a common enterprise. He was right no doubt about that; the sacred is not simply a primitive stage in our consciousness, but a structural element of the mind.

We all agreed that consciousness is a vague word overlapping with others, generating a conflict which results in a movement to higher abstractions. We used our power of playing with words because the fundamental aim of the college experience as a whole is to develop rational, critical and creative powers. Such development involves a broadening and deepening of the outlook; an awareness of one's own and other cultures.

We were ready to broaden and deepen our outlook everytime she laughed with a spasmodic shaking of her sides, and now, we were aware of her culture. She taught us that truly good work is done freely and joyfully, not in order to win a reward or a grant from the Science Foundation. The important thing is not the deed, she said, but the motivation behind it.

This was the beginning.

Then, one day, at the end of the first laughing months, she said something about the end of the world. She did not laugh and we thought that something worth being discovered had to be there.

A kind of musing soliloquy followed wherein arguments fell into patterns, unpremeditated and revealing, like the gathering of sea things washed up to the shore. The idea was that the only survivors of the great flood composed one family: that of Noah, his wife, their three sons and their wives. A discouraging environment, evil influence and misguided self-motivation turned an excellent heredity into failure. They promised to obey God. They never did. As a result, God punished the world several times via human administrations.

The prophecy of Daniel pictures a stupendous image representing the Chaldean administration, followed by the Persians, and then by the Macedonians and the Romans. The main idea is that all these administrations will be destroyed by a stone.

Here we started to giggle as a sign that nothing could be more direct, more noble and more awe-inspiring than a majestic rock, or a boldly standing block of granite. All the historians say that above all, stone is. It always exists of itself, and more important, it strikes.

She did not care about our secular comments and said that Daniel knew what the stone was. What he did not tell us is the timing.

We stopped giggling because we were used to focusing our attention anytime a problem was clearly formulated.

She brought up more details. In the prophecy the fourth administration has two legs of iron. It would be strong, as iron is strong, but divided. This was the Roman Empire with capitals in Constantinople and Rome.

We said no, because Constantinople and Rome existed in different moments in time.

She continued, saying that the ten toes, part iron, part clay, would resurrect, and seven of them would be ruled over by a whore, a daughter of ancient Babylon. Since Babylon started systematic astronomical observations, the whore has to be science, the backbone of today's outer space research.

At the beginning we had a simple expression of mirth, which soon transformed into violent laughter: a combination of spasmodic utterance of inarticulate sounds, facial distortion and shaking of the sides, given only by an acute sense of the ridiculous. Then we started thinking.

Daniel's book is ranked as the last book of the four major prophets, unique in that it is conserved in three languages. The girl was interested in the chapters setting forth revelations received in exile. The first vision tells of four monstrous beasts, the fourth being the fiercest, from which extends a horn that acts and speaks arrogantly. An angel explains that the monsters represent kingdoms. Clearly the stone has to destroy the last arrogant horn. Mention is made of four administrations symbolized by metals.

We had interminable discussions about existing interpretations of these dreams during centuries of rich cultural subsoil. We found the historical arguments that the fourth administration was that of Alexander the Great. The girl had adopted either a historically false chronology, drawn perhaps from contemporary lore, or a very old view of the world. Hesiod, one of the earliest Greek poets also mentions four ages, symbolized by the same four metals. His epic poem, *Works and Days*, traces man's decline since the Golden Age down through the Silver and Bronze, to Hesiod's own miserable era of iron.

Everything was due to Pandora, who out of curiosity opened a jar, loosing multifarious evils on mankind. Hesiod doesn't say that this jar is science.

It is strange how ancient perceptions of man and the cosmos persist in modern beliefs, and we were glad when she started talking about something else.

But later, despite our uneasiness, we constantly engaged in this debate. There was a drive towards it. Maybe the hope was that she would start to laugh again as before, when we were talking and she was listening. Something was missing, but we did not know what.

So we tried an explanation of the stone. We said that biologically man is still the great performer of the world. Therefore the stone has to be human. She agreed. We said further that the range of his adaptive potentialities has been greatly enlarged by sociocultural mechanisms that enabled him to colonize most of the earth. She agreed. We said that his adventurous spirit now tempts him to conquer other worlds, but despite the success of launching in space, his colonization days are over. She nodded. We argued that man is earthbound forever because his life is completely dependent on fresh water. The big empires were born along the great rivers. We even ventured to remember that the British empire was defined by its navy, and the same rule is valid today for the U.S. and the S.U. She did not say anything.

We continued along the same lines. Even if it is true that man is remarkably adapted to life in highly urbanized societies, the modern way of life does not contribute significantly to what we call happiness. The stone has to come from an area where people were once happy, along a great river.

The final blow was given by John Philiponus. He came up with fresh evidence from a book entitled *Pullback*, published by Vantage Press in New York. It describes a prophecy testified by Gerald O'Hara, archbishop of Atlanta, who as a nuncio in a Danubian Country, met a stygmatic who told him that the stone would come from that part of the world, and would change the face of the world.

Her laughter blew up as a thunder: incredible, violent, powerful; a sudden and involuntary tightening of the facial muscles that drew back the corners of her beautiful mouth and exposed the whitest teeth in the world.

★

Everything started when our department opened positions for a group qualified to study the new problem of artificial thinking. Although restricted to the field of computers, the problem required an interdisciplinary approach and so, in winter, we started the process of knowing each other.

The first to arrive was Dan. An expert in software, he desperately wanted a change. Anytime a new field opens its arms, there are new hopes and new energies released. Dan was convinced that pioneer research could be many times more rewarding than established routines, and without hesitation, broke previous tiring engagements. He kept only some fixed habits: boiling tea in the morning, parking his car close to the window in order to carefully watch it, or combing his hair before leaving his desk.

He liked the university campus because it was large, because the faces were not always the same, and because of the trees. Coming from the rigid world of precise engineering, where everything was supposed to follow crisp patterns, he wanted to enjoy the freedom of teaching.

Building machines is an old enterprise which gives the pleasure of being creative, of introducing new souls into the world, sometimes with amazing effects. As an old hand, Dan was a witness of many

25

breakthroughs. As a father of major achievements, he was absolutely convinced that if the thinking process can be understood and described, a machine can be built based on that clear description. He was right, because he knew the machines. He mastered many of them. He was sure that we would find the description, as in other similar cases used or misused almost everywhere.

The second to come was Andrew, a fresh Ph.D. Perfect, mild, curious, and patient, he brought the rigour of logic. He believed that everything has to be understood before attempting to introduce new souls into the world.

It was a privilege to hear his presentations. With chalk in his hand at the blackboard, his tone changed to one that was wise, prudent and clear.

Andrew was extremely artistic, and musically inclined, with a flair for literature and a poetical bent. His elegant train of deep thought never ran at breakneck speed when the destination was a decision, but it seldom went off the track. After he was finally pulled into the station he always had the right answer. Dressed like a man of distinction, he behaved like one too. He was an angel of tact, getting along with almost everyone; always married, engaged, divorced or in the middle of an important affair, he never paddled his canoe alone. He loved nothing more than betting the pros back to the cons, then switching to pitch the cons against the pros. In his eyes that was not fighting. A good intelligent argument was pure entertainment.

Alex came later.

He was a man dedicated to abstract mathematics. A gaunt, somewhat strange cranky bird with a nose like a beak jutting severely out of a lined, craggy face; he had a laughter as loud as an eruption. His voice was diffident and constrained, as though the speaker was loath to give actual sound to ideas.

Although his look was austere, even haughty, he was always speaking about beautiful women. We liked him first for his fantastic tales about chasing the girls; floating images in a collage-like picture, elements on a flat plan, some receding, some pushing forward, creating a whole that is balanced but pulsing. We liked him also for the way he handled his pipe, for his instinct for making the right professional move, and his ability to profit from the council of others. In so doing, he bypassed the mistakes that sometimes prove fatal to scientific careers.

With customary caution, he was now gradually edging his way into heavier roles, convinced that it was congenial to his temperament, and that he had the right size of voice.

Although younger, Andrew took him under his wing advising him to resist the temptation of accepting glamorous opportunities that might prove detrimental to his development in the long run. They spent hours in the library chatting with the blonde goddess, until John arrived to bewitch them with his stories.

John was the last one to come.

We nicknamed him Philiponus, the Stone. He was the one to tell us that in his grandeur, man is faced with a reality and a force that belongs to some world other than the profane one of which he is a part. He told us how Jacob went to sleep on a stone at the place where heaven and earth open onto each other, a supremely creative center. We discussed for hours the symbolism of the center in terms of embryos which proceed from the navel onward. To reach a center is to achieve a consecration, "an initiation," he said, and soon we understood that any new human enterprise must be a reconstruction of the world if it is to last and if it is to be real.

Paradise, where Adam was formed from the slime, was at the center. Paradise was set on a mountain higher than all the rest.

At that time, one couldn't have read a newspaper or a magazine without some reference to the field of computers, and the interest was certainly understandable.

It was argued, as many recall, that just as humans are expected to create their own programs, computers should be also allowed to attempt the world of reasoning without reference to any outsider.

This was perfectly possible because the machine was able to perform syllogisms: a form of reasoning in which a conclusion is reached from two different statements, as in the famous example of the philosopher Socrates who died because he was a man, and all men are mortals.

For centuries, this perfect example was given to every student in logic. John seemed to be the first to find it not so convincing. His feeling was that Socrates did not quite die. The proof was that he is still alive in the memory of all literate mankind.

He showed us that aristotelian logic imposed a crisp match between the fact that Socrates was a man, and the rule according that all men have to die. His argument was that Socrates was not simply a man, but a very wise man. Everyone agreed that men and wise men are totally different things. Our conclusion was that concepts do not respect the strange superstition known as the principle of "excluding the middle," which states that between God and men there is a vacuum, as if wise men do not exist. John's suspicion was that a better scheme could be one where God is immortal and Socrates could be godlike, therefore Socrates could be somehow immortal.

We were always amazed by his thinking, as if entering an old world full of treasures. At the beginning we believed that he didn't want to reveal his true feelings, in spite of his passion to penetrate the feelings of others. His reactions and motives were complex. It was clear for us that he responded to a kind of high calling, thanks to a rigid intellectual code which did not necessarily reflect or correspond to the one accepted by D.R.

For D.R., Aristotle was the father of today's culture. For him, culture was defined as a state of intellectual development. Although its spokesmen often sound complex, its weave of economic, social and philosophical strands are simple. Although they profess absolute confidence in God's triumph, they often exhibit a palpable fear about mankind's survival. The result is that they see conspiratorial threats all around them. Contemporary temples are more museums than shrines, where rituals do not carry the full spiritual force they once did. The religion that survives in our modern urban cultures has only private meanings: a matter between the individual and his god; more concerned with the moral than with the marvelous.

The blonde's long-lashed eyes flashed visible fire when he talked about the modern mentality, essentially Manichean, disposed to divide all reality into neat antitheses, the holy and the unsanctified; the true and the false. She answered that after all the world is an arena of conflict between evil and good, and he answered that these are vague concepts; only God knows their full meaning. We heard from John that conversion is not a radical transformation from lost to saved, but rather is a gradual transition of the heart prompted gently by God.

Then the discussion shifted toward very delicate matters. D.R. noticed the aristotelian ability to offer quick and easy solutions to complicated questions of life and belief. He spoke about some reductionist tendencies that make for speedy assimilation but shallow religion, when belief is reduced to what the Bible states without the need of historical understanding. It is as if this book had temporally preceded instead of growing out of a community of believers. His arguments were that the church and its worship cannot be reduced to the personalities and concerns of whatever little group gathers about its literal reading, as if there were not whole centuries of many other concerned readers: fellows with whom we are joined by union, blessing, and hope.

What irritated the girl was the fact that he defined hope, modern hope, as reduced to the promise of the hereafter. As if the church had no task but to await some cosmic showdown, eagerly predicted according to portents found in obscure biblical texts.

The theory of smiling says that it is possible to lose the capacity to smile spontaneously in response to a joke or an unfriendly remark. The loss of spontaneous smiling is difficult to pin down neurologically, but recent studies of stroke victims have linked it to structures in the cerebral hemispheres. It is said that this fact entails a masked-face syndrome; an emotional deadness of the face.

This is what happened: the girl turned pale, barked ha, and came up with the following text. Many people believe that death is the complete end of everything. This was unacceptable to her because it didn't make sense that certain trees can outlive intelligent men by thousands of years. Then there is the tremendous number of people

who believe that life goes on after death. Aristotle states that
contradictory views cannot be true simultaneously. But what if
these views have partial truth?

The theory of smiling says that it is possible to lose the capacity to
smile due to lesions in the part of the cerebral cortex that exerts
motor control over the facial muscles. The risorius, along with
zygomaticus major, and other more delicate sheets of tissue, must
contract in a precisely orchestrated concatenation to produce a
genuine smile. Our neural mechanism of great coordination failed
to work when we heard the last phrase. Open-mouthed D.R.
begged her to continue. She did.

God's original purpose for man, she said, was that man might live
and enjoy life on a paradise earth. We can have confidence in this
promise. It is backed by God's dependable promise that man's
enemy, death, will be destroyed. Let's say that some people are
dying and some are not. Say that those who don't die form a set. Call
it the Kingdom of God.

We didn't believe our ears. Overwhelmed by the mathematical
framework, we begged her to continue. She did.

The time of God's Kingdom to begin administering all earth's
affairs is at hand. That is no unfounded assertion. There is much
evidence backing it up. God used symbols to reveal the time of the
end and transmitted some information by means of a dream. This
manner of conveying a message is purposeful. It conceals the
meaning from those not entitled to it. The understanding of such
symbolism requires diligent study.

Her smile was automatic, almost like flinching from pain.
Hypnotized, we were ready for a diligent study. And that is what
happened.

She completely undermined our tendency to think in fixed
categories. We got rid of a mental inflexibility which is at the root of
so many misunderstandings. She pointed out that our modern
culture alters man's conception of time, and suggested a fresh study
of the relationship between history and Daniel's book.

She got to the heart of the matter and tried to eliminate non-
essential details. She spoke of the essential things, although

sometimes those of us who did not understand all the details found some connecting arguments missing.

The sine qua non of the expansion of the frontiers of science is not precise calculation, but great organizational ideas from which such calculation can arise. One arrives at new ideas by an intuitive leap and then tries to justify it by filling in the intermediate steps. Discovery is by no means a matter of only systematic deduction: it also involves insight.

The following actions were fast. Having clarified our intuitions, we were now ready to develop a theory.

First, we agreed that an end is not a short moment in time, but a period marked off by events that recur. With this, Andrew was ready to prove that the end of the world started with the French revolution. His demonstration was clear.

The main test commandments in Moses's third book, those of obedience and of faith (you shall make you no idols to bow down unto it) were followed by promise (I will give you rain in due season, and peace in the land and none shall make you afraid) and a condition (if you will not listen to me, then I will punish you seven times). Some scholars of repute say that a time unit in Leviticus has to be understood as 360 years. Therefore, the punishment becomes the withdraw of the blessings for 2520 years. Dating from the captivity of Israel, 721 B.C., that nation entered its 2520 years of punishment as foretold in Leviticus, Chapter twenty-six. This duration carries to the year 1799 A.D.

Dan started with Daniel 4:13-16. The prophet saw an immense tree chopped down at the command of one holy angel. The stump of the tree was then banded to prevent it from sprouting, and it was to remain thus banded amid the grass of one field, for seven good times. Applying the principle of a day for a year, he verified again 2520 years. Knowing the length of the times he was now in the position to investigate when they began. When Babylonians destroyed the capital of the Kingdom of God, Jehovah restrained himself from exercising his rulership in this way. This restraining is likened to the banding of

the remaining tree stump. That means that the seven times had
their start at the time when Jerusalem was destroyed. One can
establish 607 B.C. as the date of this important event. The evidence
is as follows. Babylon fell to Cyrus in the year 539 B.C. This date is
substantiated by all available historical records of ancient times. The
Bible reveals that in the first year of rule Cyrus issued a decree
permitting the exiled to return. A considerable distance in travelling
was involved. Therefore, it must have been 537 B.C. before the
builders were back in their city. In the second book of Chronicles, it
is said that a period of seventy years passed from the time of
destruction until restoration. Counting back brings us to 607 B.C.
The appointed time would 1914 A.D., the fatal year of the first
world war.

John had a different view. Modern historians, he said, do not
present 607 B.C. as the date of the event. His calculations, based on
modern historical evidence, suggested 576 B.C. This evidence was
based on testimony from eyewitnesses, and it sets out factors that
were ignored by those who pretended to understand God's
command of the course of human events. This was something new.
He confessed that his research leads to 1944 as the beginning of the
end of the world.

At this moment Alex burst out in violent laughter. His peculiar
loonlike, hysterical giggle was a sign that a spring was touched. It
was not puzzle but glee that made him whoop so loud. And glee is a
kind of pleasure towards which we have a common unsatisfied
hunger. So much of what is real and strong is pressed down out of
our consciousness by various acquired tricks, that we may properly
place truth herself besides sex as a chief source of joy. We are always
hungry for truth.

In our culture, it is stability and a resolute adherence that
insulates us from the truth. We are not always free to experience it,
either because we do not know how, or because we do not have
time. We are prisoners, usually in a mist of pretense. When
somebody shocks us with the promise of truth, the experience may
be fitly placed in comparison with the ecstasies of the saints.

When Alex started to laugh, his face widened, swelled, and became embossed, being colored by all the sanguine vapors that his skin could have. For it was only the thickness of his skin that stopped them from escaping, such was the pressure of his happiness and the power of his exhilarations.

In his treatise on Laughter, Joubert says that there is nothing that gives more pleasure and recreation than a laughing face. Joubert was right. Alex's sparkling eyes were a sign that something worth knowing was going to be revealed very soon. And when John finished his story, we saw that he was right.

★

That year, at the annual meeting of the Association for the Advancement of Science, F. Sutherland Macklem seemed to be the first to observe that the second law of thermodynamics was absorbed into science directly from the biblical narrative. In a modern interpretation, the text of Genesis says that in the beginning Elohim cut the space and the mass, and the mass was formless, and He separated the light from the darkness. He said that there will be expansion in the midsts of the flowings and there will be separation, flowings to flowings.

This is the way ancient cosmogonies introduced the intriguing notion that the light had to do with streams that imply a condensation process; and that the light preceded the sun and the stars. This nonaristotelian approach is so contrary to what we call common sense that one is forced to concur with the belief that the text was inspired by God. This was his implicit conclusion and we agreed. According to ancient Scriptures history means entropy lowering events introduced by Elohim periodically. This could be one of the reasons that God is called King of the Ages. Even D.R. was convinced that with the concept of Age the Bible can be understood as a consistent whole.

In the reference room of the library, Andrew, half-joking and half-serious, started to look carefully to find dispensations, administrations,

and distinguishable economies in the outworking of God's purpose. Soon he concluded that the two terms, age and administration, define the world as a household. The next step was to link providence and enlightenment.

We were discussing this delicate problem when the girl noticed that whenever a large and growing section of our society says yes, providence can be understood by reading the prophets, and the Book of Daniel was offered as an example. Therefore we started with it.

Daniel, the young and wise prophet, understanding visions and dreams, is supposed to know that the heavenly God makes known what shall be in the feature. There is nothing extraordinary in this. Today, anybody knowing the state equation can predict the behavior of the system. In our universities, we use the word "system" almost everyday. And not only there. We are biological systems, shaped by educational systems, coping with economical systems, and caught up in political systems. System analysts are not interested in the physical things forming the whole, but in the plan or the scheme according to which things are connected.

Daniel was a scholar trying to understand such connections. Of course, he used the language of his time, and as today, he suggested a model: an explanation describing what happens. He was stationed with his colleague Abed-Nego in the palace of Nebuchadnezzar, in training for special assignment in the Babylonian White House. Nebuchadnezzar had a dream which puzzled and moved him to tremendous concern. The dream was the model. His sorcerers, astrologers, and magicians could not tell what the dream meant. That is, the system analysts in charge failed to run the model on their computers.

In his dream, the king had seen a vast statue with a head of fine gold, breast of pure silver, belly of brass, legs of durable iron, and feet a mixture of iron and clay. Andrew noticed the key idea of two legs. At one moment in time, a stone came from heaven smashing the statue which was actually blown away by the wind. Andrew noticed the dynamic character of the model. Then the stone miraculously expanded and became a great mountain. Daniel's explanation is clear: there shall be a fourth administration, a strong one, because iron breaks to pieces and shatters all things. Andrew noticed many comments and their common mistake when considering iron as less valuable than gold.

In his turn, Daniel also had a dream. In the first year of the King Belshazzar, while lying in bed, he saw in his vision four great beasts coming out of the sea. The fourth was exceedingly strong, with ten horns. The conclusion again was that there shall be a fourth kingdom which shall devour the earth and trample it to small pieces. The ten horns were ten kings that shall arise later.

A considerable wealth of literature published over the decades easily recognizes the fourth administration as being that of the Romans. Andrew had serious doubts. For him, an administration was an ideology. Antioch IV Epihanes, the little horn of the fourth kingdom was an aristotelian. And so were the Romans.

Many interpretations of Daniel's dreams were somewhat superficial in tone and approach. The interpreters had a tendency to center too heavily on their own wishes, often to the exclusion of visible instances of God's will. They took a text, here, a word there, and a guess or two, to arrive at wanted scenarios. This wasn't a scientific approach. They failed to ask themselves what were the basic factors unleashing this or that particular administration.

The question of whether the study of prophecies had utilitarian value, is a vexed one. We were sure that so far as history goes, we can learn from the past. The past states that the immediate causes of the imperial rivalries lie in greed and in fear. Andrew came with documents from the library showing that nearly all governments are convinced, with different degrees of enthusiasm, that to remain a great nation or to become one, they must colonize (The Waganda are clamouring for shoes, stockings, and opera glasses, and are daily developing fresh wants, Cecil Rhodes' brother wrote hopefully of Uganda).

The library was full of books written by abstract historians, who were sure that England reached a colonial settlement with France, and made an agreement on several outstanding imperial issues with Russia, all as a result of the German decision to embark on naval expansion. This effort to become another empire, bearing the white man's burden as praised by Kipling, lies in opposition to Joseph Chamberlain's warning that the British race is the greatest of governing races.

Andrew preferred the nonabstract historians. One day he came with a book written by Birmingham, who states that everyday Jacob Schiff, the New York banker, pronounced a grace to our God and Father who has not only given us life, but also gives us daily bread, blessing us with His mercy so that we may be able to share our own plenty with those less fortunate. Frieda, his daughter, wrote that his hatred of imperial Russia prompted him to take the great risk of financing the Japanese war. Late in the summer of 1915, Britain's financial wizard, Lord Rufus, arrived in New York to negotiate an allied loan. The Allies could have their money if France and Britain would give Jacob Schiff their assurance in writing that not one cent of the loan would be given to Russia, because he could not stultify himself by aiding those who had tortured his people and will continue to do so, whatever professions they may make in their hour of need.

Andrew was absolutely convinced that a systematic discussion of any one of these topics could constitute a major contribution to the theory of empires, dispensations, and God's will.

Alex started to laugh. His heart, struck by what seemed enjoyable to it, expanded thirstily, as if to embrace the generous ideas presented. In this dilation, great amounts of blood poured forth, and on his face appeared evident signs of rejoicing: an open countenance, a shining, clear, and taut forehead, sparkling eyes, reddening cheeks, and a drawing back of the lips.

When Andrew mentioned that even Lenin suspended the central principle of advancing world revolution in order to expediate obtaining financial credits and encourage businessmen to invest in concessions from which they were promised large profits, Alex widened his mouth further in convulsions. His breast heaved, and his voice became interrupted. For a long time the veins in the throat became seriously enlarged, while his arms shaked and his legs danced. He coughed, perspired and felt pain. His laughter was interminable.

Then, John entered the scene.

Anyone reading this who knew John, (and many will, because he was so widely known and respected), will recall how that tall, imposing man could go completely out on historical research. In fact when he spoke, he held his listeners spellbound, because he was spellbound with his facts. History, aside from applied mathematics, was his life. We were to work together over a joy-filled period of five years, dumbfounded at his vast knowledge. So far as we knew, he was the only person who could, without glancing at anything, give you in superbly chosen, fluent language, the complete history of the Roman Administration. Being inclined to believe the less abstract historians, and John was one of them, we asked him what happened at its end. This time his story was long.

It was founded shortly before our era by God's grace, to unify his people in preparation for the advent of the stone; its eastern half survived for a thousand years after the western half had crumbled into various feudal kingdoms. The eastern realm was more civilized and its emperors were more inclined towards nonaristotelian thinking, being therefore more skillful in fending off the invaders. With such advantages, the emperors nourished the dreams of subduing the western barbarians, the addicted aristotelians.

Andrew noted the legs.

Alex started to laugh. Dan was sure that his laughter was not necessarily malign or irreverent, but it was of a quality incompatible with that fixed concentration of serious feelings which we call devout. John continued the story.

The Fourth Crusade resulted in the fall of Constantinople to the shrewd Venetian bankers, but the empire was recaptured by the exiles who slowly in two hundred years, changed it into little more than a large city-state, besieged from all sides.

Andrew noted the power of he exile. Alex noted the decay after the periods of high level functioning and grumbled at the low consideration Dan had for him. He argued that the essence of laughter is flexibility, not fixation. Its food is not unity but variety. Laughter he said, is superior in its hospitality toward the continual arrivals of truth. John continued the story.

When Constantinople was captured it was almost deserted. The conqueror began to repeople it by transferring Macedonians from around Salonika. The rulers were wise enough to follow God's will, and the Macedonian colony experienced freedom of trade, language, and worship. Those who did not trust all these freedoms went into exile, where their gold made them accepted, or across the big river Danube to wait better times; to watch and to wait.

Andrew noted again the exile. Alex, still grumbling, said that for science laughter is a congenial companion. Not only is laughter independent of any particular belief or intellectual commitment, and so not hostile to the mood of inquiry, but in softening the rigor of the passions it removes the chief obstacle to the process of verification. Dan answered him with a "shut up." John continued undisturbed.

The influential transdanubians were pursuing a policy of their own which was not to disrupt the existing system but to take it over as an ongoing concern. They always denied the Russian right to interfere in the Balkans which was invoked as a result of a marriage between the niece of the last Roman Emperor and the great prince Ivan, the first ruler to call himself czar.

When the days of the great sultans were over, amidst the ramshackle of their once efficient administration system, the Macedonian colony climbed the rungs of the power. By the eighteenth century, they had done this so successfully that four of the great offices of state, dragoman of the Palace, dragoman of the fleet, and governors of each of the two transdanubian provinces were virtually their preserves. These provinces were ancient colonies established by Rome, still preserving its language.

Like two cultured pearls produced in a shell into which a piece of grit has been introduced, Alex was prompt to observe. Dan did not

like this intervention. Alex said that it is the continual effort of science
to get rid of valuations where it can. Humor is the very act of taking
these valuations lightly. John went further.

These dragomans were endowed with great political shrewdness.
They accompanied administrators, courtiers, and all kinds of adventurers
who for two hundred years, came to seek their fortune in a rush
comparable to the one which attracted prospectors to the Californian
shores. This is how Kasotti arrived: young, penniless, handsome;
ready to marry a wife with some means.

Turning from generalities to real facts made all the difference in the
world. Alex didn't laugh any more. Dan didn't say anything. John
continued without interruptions.

An issue of bonds, the first ever made in this part of the world, in
payment of expropriated mortgaged estates was thrown into the
market by Prince Cuza in 1864. Since no landowner could believe in
the values of these pieces of paper, they sold out in a breath, and
Kasotti bought all he could of these despised chits. Within a couple of
years his investment had increased tenfold.

On a trip to Paris, he was caught in the siege of 1870, and instead of
fleeing, remained there to try his luck on the slumping stock
exchange; where the French rents were falling to nothing. He
managed to borrow a million francs from Rothschild, bought state
shares and by 1872 the government bonds were par.

When he died, his daughter Helen Kasotti became a wealthy
Romanian heiress and married a highbrow. Her mother-in-law,
Maria Manescu was a daughter of Dr. Apostol Arsaki who, in the
1820s, fleeing from the Turkish-ruled Salonika towards more lenient
lands, had gone on foot over the mountains with two children carried
in twin baskets hung on either side of a mule.

The father-in-law, Vacarescu, also married an heiress, whose
premature death had left him free to indulge his mad whims. He
converted the better part of her fortune into cash, and packing loads
of gold ducats into a specially built yellow coach, sallied abroad. When
the funds ended, he returned to his estate only to find it neglected and
ruined by his trusted bailiffs. With what barely remained he gave

Theodore, then in Potsdam, a high education.

A few years after his marriage, Theodore, as aide-de-camp of Prince Cuza, entered a conspiracy to replace him by Prince Charles. The plot succeeded mainly because the conspirators, on entering his bedroom, found Cuza in such company that he could not call for his guard in order to shield the reputation of his mistress, a well-known royal and beautiful lady.

The new Prince immediately appointed Colonel Vacarescu as Marshal of the Court. Only when he became involved in an affair with an actress, was he compelled to resign his court office, but even then he was appointed Ambassador to Vienna.

Radu, his son and secretary during the sojourn in Vienna, married Helen Kasotti, and in 1908 Europe became aware that his daughter Ana Maria was an available bride.

In June 1910, Ana Maria, after turning down a proposal of His Royal Highness Don Jaime of Bourbon, Duke of Madrid, (claiming as his due the whole crown of Spain, and ready to fight for its total redemption) was married to John Calimachi.

His name had originally been Calmash. At the end of the seventeenth century, Tudor Calmash, a simple landowner, had high ambitions for his sons. Gabriel entered the church and ended as a Bishop. John was sent to Constantinople to acquire knowledge on world trade, international politics and intrigue. From student, he rose to be Great Dragoman to the Sultan. Then, having gained enough wealth and contacts necessary for bribes, he worked his way to the nomination as prince of his country. His outstanding ability gained him the confidence of the sultan, warded off rivalry and silenced the slander. As a ruler, he died in his bed, a rare feat for those princes whose lives usually ended drowned in the sea tied in a bag, beheaded, or starved to death in a dungeon. Four of his descendants had at different periods and with different fates, occupied thrones.

The honeymoon lasted two years. Norway's midnight sun was the first aim, to be reached by meandering routes. The first world war caught them during the second race at the Austrian Derby in Vienna. Due to the assassination of the Heir Apparent to the

Imperial Throne, His Imperial Highness Archduke Ferdinand Franz, the race was suspended.

John Philiponus told us that this story can be found in a book entitled *Yesterday Was All Mine* published by McGraw-Hill in New York after the second world war. Princess Ana Maria, the author, did not tell why they rushed home, but an answer can be found in another book entitled *The Last Real Romantic*, written by another beautiful woman from New York who dedicated five hundred pages to Marie, the beautiful granddaughter of the powerful Empress of the British Empire.

Here D.R. noticed John's erudition when the subject was a beautiful woman. Something was in the air. His sardonic expression was proof. This sarcastic remark was intended to wound some undeclared feelings. The word sarcasm means a tearing of the flesh like dogs, and may well be considered a function of the teeth rather than of the lips. The cynic attitude of D.R. derived its existence from the dog.

Laughter itself is not an act of rejection but of acceptance. Laughter is delight, not derision, as anyone would be convinced by observing the light in the beautiful eyes of the beautiful goddess completely absorbed in John's story. He continued.

No one in the English Royal Family understood why Princess Marie was not given to her cousin Prince George, who wanted her as his wife. The fact is that she married Ferdinand Victor, the Heir Apparent of the Romanian throne. Another fact was that she was a virgin.

Dan mentioned how today sexuality is openly discussed in the media, turning promiscuous sex into public acceptance. It may be questioned whether as few as one percent of young brides go to the altar as virgins. Marriage for much of society is on the way out. Alex giggled a little. D.R. grinned from ear to ear. Patiently, slowly, John continued the story.

This is how Marie met Prince Stirbey, whose father reigned once before Cuza. He was a cousin of Ana Maria, one of those who wanted to resurrect the Eastern Roman Empire.

Nobody laughed. Our attention was totally captured. John started to go at a good pace.

One of the richest and most powerful men in the world, he had an intuitive grasp of reality and a great facility for getting things done. By looking carefully around, Stirbey came to the conclusion that change was the name of the game. With accurate, shrewd judgment, he foresaw that Austria, Russia, and Turkey would be subdued. Ever since the early 1900s there had been a gradual shifting of power. After the French Revolution, the world money power shifted from Paris to London. Then, in 1914, New York replaced London as the world's financial navel. These global changes altered the way the great powers jockeyed for control in the Balkans.

The assassination of the Archduke Ferdinand Franz did not shake Bucharest as it did governments throughout the world. The members of the Royal Family were also at the Sunday horse races when by telegram, the tragedy was delivered to the old king who died without understanding what was going to happen. King Ferdinand took his oath at his turn, while the new Queen Marie stood to one side with her four children, as a sign that everything would go well. The war came and the Queen embraced it.

By entering that cruel war on the right side, the Queen was in fact serving notice to the neutral spectators that the most formidable uncommitted nation in Europe felt certain what cause would win. With the postwar kingdom doubled in size, Queen Marie saw herself being invested with tiara and mantle, although the borders of her enlarged realm had not yet been settled. Coached by Stirbey, she got in touch with the world leaders in order to prove the validity of her claims. In her diary, Marie admits that she obtained what Stirbey wished: the success of a magnificent cause. While traveling extensively, she wrote him long letters about the darkening of the international scene, and about her longing to once again have their gallops through the woods.

She returned hom in triumph, and accordingly Stirbey changed some of their plans. Previously, during the war, the heir to the throne Crown Prince Charles II, met Jeanne Marie Valentine Lambrino, known as Miss Zizi. She claimed as forebears a ninth-century emperor of Byzantium, married to a daughter of the emperor Charlemagne. Small and dark, blessed with all kinds of gifts, subtlety, and a vivid imagination, she was a perfection which made the crown prince go across the border, find a priest, and get married.

But after the triumph, the strategy was totally different. First, Princess Mignon was settled on the Yugoslavian throne. Then, when Greece became a kingdom, Princess Elisabeth married its Crown Prince George. Then, Prince Charles II married Helen of Greece. In a few months, Marie had procured for her family a monopoly of the Balkans. The idea of a coronation came about soon.

Queen Marie was turned to the splendours of the Byzantine rites. She asked all the women in the procession to wear gold, silver, and mauve. Over her long straight dress she hung diamonds, and a gigantic sapphire. Her crown was copied from one worn by Princess Despina, the beautiful wife of a happy sixteenth-century prince. Set with rubies, emeralds, turquoise, and giant moonstones, the gold crown weighted four pounds and had huge jeweled pendants that hung down over the ears. The Queen wore it over a delicate veil of gold mesh. This was the peak. When Prince Charles II became King, he got rid of Stirbey.

Without a moderating influence upon him the young king exhibited a kind of Machiavellian gusto. He was ready to commit violent and unjust acts, and his time lent itself to their commital.

The Roman Empire died August 1944, maybe because august means majestic. The fact is testified by Bishop and Crayfield in a book titled *The Russians Astride the Whole Balkans.*

Here John stopped for a while. As always Dan was open-mouthed, while Alex puffed on his pipe. Andrew was sure that each generation has to rewrite history. It was too long a time since the basic narrative had been rewritten to meet the rapidly changing needs of the new generations. In the twenty-first century such an account must constitute a systematic introduction to the collective memory of that tradition which we are being asked to defend. The girl didn't say anything. She was impatient to hear the rest of the story. He went on with his outline.

One of the authors left the U.S. in 1941 for Lisbon, Paris, and Berlin.

By renewing an old acquaintance with Karl Bodenschatz, a Luftwaffe General, and liason officer between Hitler and Goering, he established what was without doubt the closest link to the Reichmarshal. Later, with the U.S. entry into the war, he left Germany by employing a ruse and entered the Romanian Kingdom, where he volunteered for both the British and the American Services.

Bucharest was then the center for Abwehr and Gestapo operations throughout southeastern Europe. It was a spy center like Lisbon, where intelligence was filtered by the long way through France and through Spain. Information out of Romania came directly and could be relayed to Allied agents in Turkey with relative ease.

Bishop and Crayfield say that the conquest of Romania was accomplished by Air Forces. The bombers attacked so hard and so relentlessly, that this country, bleeding, beaten and exhausted, sank to her knees. Others say that plotters, convinced that their country entered that war on the wrong side, begged for some mercy. What is certain is that whole sections of cities were leveled to deserts of debris. Great oil refineries were blown up and tumbled into a mass of twisted dead steel. Oil storage plants were destroyed. Railway yards became silent crater fields, strewn with wrecked cars that looked like corpses of strange monsters. Bridges, broken and useless, no longer stretched over rivers. Flares and fires, searchlights and tracers illuminated the nights, turning them into weird days, and the days were made gloomy and dark from smoke and dust.

"The Stone," we said, right on cue.

John didn't answer and continued to purr.

Stirbey went to Turkey to find out how his country could quit the war. He even permitted himself to be photographed in Cairo on his secret mission. A Swiss illustrated weekly published that photograph with a caption telling all about his intentions, negotiations, and hopes. He had something of great value to sell. But he did not come home with promises, guarantees and encouragement. Boiled down and stripped of moral support, he died a year later.

He never knew that Major Charles Hostler had arrived and that in his wake came Major Hall and Lieutenant William Hamilton attempting to get in touch with his people. Heading for the list were the disgruntled plotters of August, for they were angry at being deprived of the fruits of their victory.

As all the meandering streams of Romania ultimately flow into the Danube, so Hall and Hamilton drifted into the one and only catch-all of political people, the discarded putchists.

The first meeting took place in the home of Lieutenant Colonel Wilcox. A second one was held in the house of a King's friend, Baron Moscony Styrcea. The third and most important meeting took place in the partly bombed palace of Stirbey. Plane for a resistance movement with foreign aid were discussed, and short stenographic notes of the proceedings were made. For safety, Ioana Bujoi, ex-wife of Prince Ghika, known as the blue princess, took all the notes. Nobody knows, even today, why in twenty-four hours the plot was discovered. Indictments were made and purge trials followed.

Dramatic and tense moments highlighted the trial. One such moment came when Styrcea admitted that the officers told him that they were giving consideration to political processes started after the war, but they were surprised at the passivity of the opposition. Hall and Hamilton said they were acting on high authority for a new independent service which had the duty to coordinate all intelligence of the other departments, and report directly to high ranking leaders.

A little bit puzzled, the girl asked for an explanation. She wanted to know where the legs were that are clearly stated in the first part of Daniel's prophecy. Nobody dared to venture hasty conclusions that could be regretted. Later, at an author's evening organized by the PEN center, illuminating geopolitical thoughts made the problem even more complicated. The speaker, a journalist of repute, gave us the following lecture.

When the cold war began, everyone believed that all our problems were the fault of the evil empires. There was a reason for this big scare. World War Two made prosperous these empires which had been undergoing depression for years. In order to maintain a general prosperity, they decided to become the unvanquished world's policemen. (This is the reason for all arms races. We are put on a permanent wartime economy, which is why a third or so of government revenue is constantly being siphoned off to pay for what is euphemistically called defense, the perenial shield against the barbarians.) Then, the money shifted from New York to Tokyo. Now the long-feared asiatic colossus takes its turn as world leader, and we, the white race, become the yellow man's burden. The foreseeable future could be asiatic; some combination of Japan's advanced skill with China's resourceful landmass. Europe and the U.S. will then be simply irrelevant to the world. Europe began as the relatively empty uncivilized land west of Asia. Then the western hemisphere became the wild west of Europe. The sun is moving constantly to the West. There is only one way out now. The alliance of the great powers, the U.S. and the S.U., will double the strength of each and have an opportunity to survive.

It was Alex who observed that this new U.S.-S.U. administration, with symmetrical legs, fits Daniel's prophecy. His face widened, swelled and was embossed, becoming visibly colored. His sparkling eyes were a precise sign that something worth our attention had been found.

The sharp, explosive, barklike laughter of the girl convinced us that this was the most unheard of thing she had ever heard of. We were sure that her laughter grew out of a sense of the misfortune of mankind which does not know what is going to happen. Our loud, boisterous, laughter was like that of the gods in Homer's epics. We laughed, and laughed, and laughed, the veins in our throats became enlarged. We couldn't stop our laughter for hours, days and weeks.

The result was totally unexpected. We didn't need much effort to clear up the mystery of the topic sentence in the proposal to the Science Foundation. We wrote that we wanted to explore a conceptual framework needed to examine the process we call qualitative change, based on the fact that all contradictions are reconciled in higher synthesis.

"Amazing, fantastic, sensational," shouted Alex. His voice, with its hint of raspiness and lilting, became steeped in an angelic intonation of laughter which we took as proof that something worthy of applause had been introduced into our environment. And he was right.

The second law of what we call cybernetics was just absorbed into science from the biblical narrative.

★

Like all sponsors, The Science Foundation was generous but demanding. They accepted our proposal and asked for a report after one year. Like all those engaged in research, we did not come easily to terms with what to write in the report.

That summer we were supposed to meet a new deadline and finish the text. This report had to be intelligible enough to a scientifically literate reader, and should include the findings and the possible implications, stated concisely, for publication in the Annals. This publication was used to answer inquiries by distinguished nonscientists as to the significance of the research, since they were the investors.

On the longest day of the year, in June, we started a chain of discussion meant to reveal what must be put in the report.

There was a decided difference between us, as we were men of decided opinion. Our decision to postpone vacations was like an answer to a high calling. The campus was empty. Students, teachers, their noise and their smell, everything disappeared. We were alone; we and the librarians, the only survivors. Now we were ready again to count the hairs that make a bald man hairy: challenging the Aristotelian wisdom which demands that each case, bald and not bald, must be crisp; the middle being excluded.

For more than two years, we carefully analysed the use of vague concepts such as good, bad, sweet, gorgeous, and divine. For more than two years, we saw that there is no determined point at which a transition from a clear to a borderline case could occur. We saw that the question of truth or falsity is undecideable. We saw that words are dangerous things to handle. We saw all these things; now we were ready to write what we saw. The problem was how.

The Science Foundation cautioned us against being late. We were cautioned by our instincts not to drive fast.

From the beginning of our research, we obtained many proofs that science distinguishes between practical facts expressed in vague, everyday language, and theoretical facts expressed in more vague, technical jargon. The confidence in the truth of a vague statement may be justified just because of its vagueness. It is precisely such vagueness which makes abstract concepts compatible with a wide range of facts.

Later, we discovered that science acquires prestige at the expense of the vagueness of natural languages. There is a balance between certainty and precision. One is increased to the detriment of the other.

For more than two years, we believed that we could capture the secret of vagueness. That summer was a deadline. Having gathered useful material for our subject from here and there, and having culled appropriate passages from the intellectual meadows of our peers, we tried to consolidate them into a well written report for submittal to the revered Science Foundation.

When we read the first draft of the report, we saw repetitions, overlapping accounts, clumsy transitions, dullness yielding haphazardly to high drama, sudden shifts from bookkeeping details to metaphors, and a great number of vague concepts. Taken together, they gave the work an impersonal structure which seemed to be that of the research itself.

For two years, we had traveled a deserted and untrodden road, praying that we may have the power of God as our co-worker. At the beginning we were unable to discover even the bare tracks of those who followed the same path before us. Later we discovered brief remarks through which, in one way or another, left partial accounts of their research. Finally, we discovered voices crying out from on high, as from lofty watch towers.

In the library we found papers and books dealing with the paradox of the hips. There, in ancient books, it was written that everybody can distinguish beautiful women from those who are not. And we ourselves verified that no goddess stops being sweet because one tenth of an inch is added to her breasts or her hips. Arguing in the same way, one can reach the absurd conclusion that a beautiful woman is ugly, for if the first argument is accepted, so is a second, in a chain without end.

We laughed as always when our intelligence found itself in the presence of things that are and that are not. The paradox of the hips awoke peals of violent laughter. The conflict between what is thought and what is perceived, and the victory of perception over thought, with its resolution by laughter, convinced us that abstract concepts cannot get down to fine shades of difference of the concrete. This was what we felt when evaluating multifarious hips. It was spring when we met and had lunch at a table close to the window, observing without being observed, the university womanhood parading in front of our own private grandstand; the trim, the taut, and the wholly toned. We were blessing the smooth, firm shaped, sensible legs, walking in sandals and cut-off jeans. Some are sweet and some are sophisticated, and these are vague concepts. We were noting also that such is the content of the mental life of the Hemingway hero. Everyday he gets beaten into a servile pulp by his own mechanical reflex which is constantly busy registering and reacting to violent stimuli, only to cover them with vague labels. With such labels we built short conclusions. To the mind of modern goddesses, legs, like busts, are power points which she has been thought to tailor as part of her success kit. She swings the legs from the hip with masculine drive. She knows that a long-legged bird can go places. Her legs are display. This is the truth.

There at that table we questioned the truth, and speculated about its degrees. We jumped further into the symbol usage. D.R. of the

Apes supposed evolutionary reasons why women evolved hemispherical breasts like buttocks. According to him, a feature survived if it helped its possessors to transfer genes to the next generation. D.R. was sure that women did not stand on two legs from the beginning, and he analyzed their rump signals.

In the spring the living, physical beauty of a campus full of young flowers is really overwhelming. As one marvelously formed performer moves, another comes into view. Their deportment is proud and graceful, almost an idealization of what the human form is meant to achieve in harmonious symmetry.

Andrew was too clever not to observe that we have to look for symmetry in our text. The statue in Daniel's dream was symmetrical, with two legs. Dan murmured something about the department of physics looking for symmetry to confirm the probability of their formulations. They also use two legs: matter and antimatter, waves and particles.

There, in the spring, the girls were supported on long, powerful legs. Their hips waggled when they walked. Their bearing indicated no awareness.

In the middle of May, schedules were hectic, and we didn't have the time to put our ideas on paper. Dan confessed pessimistic views, a vicious circle in which society and culture are located. Culture is possibly only at the expense of sex. In this way it is not only organically tied to misfortune, but also doomed to destruction. He spoke at length about the role of the death instinct, a view that leaves to life only the choice to the right path toward death.

Andrew laughed and said "Bullshit. That is nothing other than Buddhism, the doctrine of the four noble truths that existence is suffering, its cause is senseless desire, and the goal is complete extinction. In Nirvana there is no death, birth, distinction, oneness, coming in, going forth. All things are empty. They have no beginning, no end, they are not imperfect, nor perfect. Therefore, Oh Daniputta, there is no form, no perception, no name, no concept, no knowledge, no sex."

Alex noticed wisely that glamour bears witness to the presence of the ideal at the heart of the real. And D.R. said that nothing in the world can be compared with a beautiful woman, a truth to be verified every fall and every spring, in any grassy area of the various quads of the campus, where the fauna mixed with flora; where the squirrels witnessed our academic and nonacademic discussions, where we questioned the reason why God punished man with sexual reproduction.

Dan spoke for hours about those cells that live, grow and separate by fission or budding. They never die, except accidentally. They are immortal, like water. They go on untiringly, doubling their number. Adam was meant for asexual reproduction. The appearance of Eve meant the appearance of death, the rejoining of the inorganic universe from which Adam had miraculously emerged.

Faced with disturbing views, we took precautions. Back in the room of the old department of physics, we could concentrate on more theoretical aspects.

First we started to joke about those poor teachers who believed in particles called electrons swirling around a nucleus in predictable orbits, even if they could not be seen.

They were in the realm of what the imagination could conceive, John said. "Bullshit," replied Dan. "How can you conceive an electron as a mathematical point with no volume and occupying no space, but simultaneously filling the space surrounding the nucleus of the atom?"

"This is a world where things are not things. It is a world where words do not mean what they seem to mean."

"Like the U.S.-S.U. administration which is and is not," ventured shyly from the pipe a still dreaming Alex.

We laughed for hours. Surely, laughter has to be related to logic. As usual the laughter came whenever we traced a new syllogism with two premises, one undisputed and one unexpected.

D.R. expressed scorn in a sneering fashion.

Dan noticed that today the physicists are in the realm of poets and priests.

D.R. curled his lip back to bare the once canine teeth, although it has been a long time since man, in his endless armament race, has considered his denture.

Although Dan did not like D.R. (and he was not the only person we ever met who did not) they concluded that a world where things are and are not is a nonaristotelian world, and all those seeking oneness are nonaristotelians. An example is the new breed of physicists called symmetrists who look for elegance and simplicity to confirm the probability of their formulations.

In July, with the materials in our hands, we endeavoured to write. By arranging all the parts so as to form one connected whole, we tried to combine a narrative of day-to-day life with the play of light and shade, without which no portrait can be a good likeness. We did not know that the particular method in which we treated the parts had ever been adopted before. What is certain is that each part was pruned of everything that seemed irrelevant to our purpose, of everything that we thought could be omitted. Every sentence that remained added something, however small, to the means of forming a conclusion. Finally, we decided to say a word of apology for what might appear to be undue detail. After all, recollections of conversation are seldom to be trusted in the absence of notes made at the time. We decided to include these notes as much as possible. The value of spoken words depends so much upon the tone and the circumstances which gave rise to their utterance. We decided to inform the readers about these circumstances. Otherwise, he or she will never understand what happened, and why, and where, and when, and who were the authors.

The spoken words often mislead as much as they enlighten, when in the process of repetition, they take color from another mind. To avoid misunderstandings, we decided to give all the details, at the expense of length, and taking the risk of being accused of undue verbiage. Only in this way can our work be encountered by direct experience. We thought it will be read and read, generation after generation, each one mounting new interpretations, thus keeping it alive in the libraries.

It is true that all interpretations depend upon the interpreters, but new interpretations will pull back towards equilibrium. In this point, our remarks will be less detailed, but they will be more certain. Each detail will be perceived less distinctly, but the principal facts will be described with more certainty. The details of the immense picture will be lost in the shade, but a clear idea of the entire report will be better conceived. We decided to supply all the details and leave the reader to find the shape of the whole.

Then the earth took a sudden new turn. Dan came with a new message, and our report was put aside. The message was about Einstein, his idol; the intellectual and political rebel who changed the very fabric of physics, motivated by a profound conviction that beauty was there waiting to be discovered.

The message was short. Only one sentence, intelligible enough to a scientific, literate mind which can understand everything by getting a glimpse into it. The sentence included the finding and the implication. Einstein was married to Mileva Maric, his Serbian classmate; the Romanian Solovine was the best man, and Helen Dukas, whose name was clearly one of a Byzantine imperial descent, was his secretary for more than twenty-five years.

This was too much. Even D.R. burst into violent laughter. His head jutted severely out from the body, and his facial distortions made him look like a bird.

Dan did not give up, because he was not the type. He was right, because what followed was worth our attention.

He told us that the eminent physicist was accused of running an espionage ring.

Miraculously, our laughing stopped, and we were ready to listen. All little boys like thrillers, and this one was supposed to have one thousand and five hundred pages, a figure discovered by Dan in *The Nation*, where it was written. The Bureau of Investigation had accumulated data for over twenty-three years, suggesting concern about Einstein's activities at very high levels. Dan's story was terrible.

In 1950, Emma Rabbeis from Berlin sent a letter to the Department of State in which she claimed to be in a position to make very positive statements concerning Einstein's activity during the years before the war. Although the accusations were dismissed, the cover letter to the report notes that Einstein's Berlin Office could have been used as a drop for telegraph messages being sent directly to Moscow. An unnamed source claimed later that the messages were interpreted by a chief secretary, and that Einstein might have been unaware of this, since she forwarded the telegrams before he could have seen them. But, when his secretary was on vacation for several weeks, Einstein was allegedly handing the messages along with the rest of the mail. That allegation led to a series of investigations intended to locate nice people who lived near him at the time. That was a difficult task, since most of them had been killed in the war, or were missing, living in the eastern sector of Berlin. The suspicion eventually turned towards Helen, who was interviewed by experienced agents. She was friendly and quite sincere in her answers. She stated that Einstein worked only at home and had no office during his residence in Berlin. Her recollection in itself tended to discredit the allegations that Einstein had a staff of secretaries and typists. At the same time, the assistant commissioner of the Immigration Service replied that the information available indicated that this naturalized person, notwithstanding his world-wide reputation, may be properly investigated, and the investigation should be conducted to determine whether there are activities in the past of the subject which might justify a suit to cancel his citizenship.

Alex did not have the power to shut up and whooped that Emma was a bitch and had a spite against Albert, known as an incurable womanizer. D.R. said that, divorced from its roots in man's biological function, love is tragic. If paradise is sought anywhere but on earth, the result is death. The divine in human form is the ecstasy of orgasm. In any other form, it exists only in angels and saints. He felt great Albert was simply a martyr, and he started to tell us his own story with his Emma, a cunning and vicious bitch who twisted everything. He told us how he wanted to screw her good and long, and make her crawl to him because he could do it so good. He wanted her to chase him, crying and pleading, and he would have grooved her and teased her, and built and built until he would have made her scream. She was such a strong wily bitch, who would have skinned his balls. He was afraid of her. He knew many Emmas, and he was afraid of them all. They are all bitches.

Dan said, "give me a break, you hussy," and continued.

In 1932, a small group of patriotic old women objected loudly to his being allowed to enter the U.S. His response was caustic. Never before, he wrote, did he experience from the fair sex such energetic rejection of all advances, or if he had, then certainly never from so many at once. However, he was convinced that the vigilant ladies were right. One should not open one's doors to a man who is so wicked as to reject wars, except the unavoidable war with his wife. Hearken therefore, to your patriotic and clever folk, and remember that mighty Rome was also once saved by the cackling of its faithful sweet geese.

Finally, Dan checked and found that in June 1932 Einstein wrote that he tried very hard to form his own judgement of what was happening in the S.U. He had reached some rather somber conclusions. He saw that at the top there appeared to be a personal struggle in which all means were used by power-hungry individuals. At the bottom, there seemed to be a complete suppression of power. He wondered what life was worth under such conditions.

Puzzled, we tried to understand why, after all, he was investigated. Andrew came up with the idea that the eminent physicist was persecuted for his nonaristotelian logic. His theory ran counter to the classical Euclidean structure in the geometry booklet. Central to his own theory was the denial of the strict validity of the Pythagorean theorems. John decided that Albert The Great was a stone.

Amazed, Alex burst into barklike laughter. The exhalations were enormous and irregular, pumping the air around him. His face swelled and widened; his lips drew back, the veins became enlarged, and his body shook.

We were sure that this laughter grew out of a sense of the misfortune of the old ladies, and of Emma who did not understand our Great Einstein.

Only D.R. insisted that Albert did not understand them, and what he meant was that many ladies tend to be schizoid. He used the term to refer to a loss of self. His resulting inhibited laugh was translated into a shaking of the sides. John said something like wait a minute, the historian was right to say that men have never adored stones simply as stones. The devotion in every case is fastened on something which

which the stone incorporated and expressed.

For many days, we labored over this question. Like mathematics, the physical sciences once seemed to promise an objective, viewer-independent account of physical phenomena. Einstein put an end to this dream. According to him, time would not pass at all on a clock traveling at the speed of light, and when under such a condition the length of a measuring rod would shrink. Time and space ultimately mean nothing except in relation to each other. Without universal time, other seemingly self-evident truths, such as causality, lose empirical validity as well. Albert was a destroyer of myths.

The finding by one observer that a mother preceded her child is ambiguous, since a second observer moving relative to the first might find that the child preceded the mother. Right? "Right," answered Dan. Therefore a mother can be a virgin. Right? "Right," answered Dan. Mind over matter. Great Albert knew more things than we do. We felt the urge to communicate our new finding.

Our room was close to the library. This is the main reason why we were there almost every afternoon. Those who were malevolent towards us made allegations that we were there simply because of the blonde goddess. But they could not substantiate them.

They probably listened to our snickers, titters, and guffaws, and probably they barked about her beauty and her charms; how we prostrated ourselves before her violent fit of laughter, and how a librarian was adorned as a queen by grave teachers, known as Ph.D.s, and victorious researchers. But the truth was that our blonde friend was the only one able to find and to understand old documents about the Academy of Plato, and about Petrus Sabatius who in the sixth century pulled it down.

Petrus Sabatius was like a stone. He brought the Academy to its knees. The surviving sect of Aristotelians, whom Aristotle would have blushed to acknowledge, extravagantly mingled superstition with the practice of magic. They did not believe in a world which is and is not, in a God who is known and unknown. Great Albert did. He also brought the Academy to its knees. The Great Albert was also a stone.

That was the conclusion of Dan. Alex made sounds and movements of the face showing amusement. D.R. said "Hey stone," and kept joking in the same vein for a while.

There is truth in the dictum, probably of De Quincey, that of all the bores, the most insufferable is the teller of the same joke. He is a nuisance that should be put down by cudgelling, or any mode of abatement, as summarily as man would combine to suffocate a vampire or a mad-dog. But Dan didn't say anything. For him all the failures and the imperfections in the bitter current of time's reality were a part of God's eternal perfection, and so he made himself happy to suffer.

Alex declared that failure and imperfections are funny, and he accomplished the same thing. For him humor was like religion: it fills a similar function in relieving us of intolerable poignancies.

They both departed from John, but they departed in contrary directions. John was also inclined toward compliance. He was ready to appreciate the good side of people and things, rather than to pronounce harsh judgements. He said that probably the aristotelians were most insufferable because they were the tellers of the same joke, a nuisance that was put down not by cudgelling but by stones. Look at me child, through art we are able to see, in even familiar scenes, things we hadn't noticed or fully comprehended previously. In heretofore uncharted expanses of the universe, the secret worlds within are sometimes revealed to us with an almost painful clarity. An artist is not an aristotelian. He works with shades. He is not happy with black and white only.

Precision may be serviceable within a limited domain, but it breaks down if we ask too much of it.

D.R. didn't curl his lip. This time he didn't bare the canine. Nobody will ever know why.

It is hard to write about D.R. with fairness. It will not be endured by the reader to mention our surprise. The fact is that the lack of his derisive laughter and disgusted scowls was a shock.

★

We read so many books of such fundamental grasp and insight, as cannot be expected to appear more than once or twice in a century; so many papers in so many journals published in so many countries and so many reports written by internationally noted fellows. We read every word of them with gratitude and sense of enrichment, that it seemed a mere trifle to systemize our long hours of discussions and conclude in a convenient manner in order to write our report to the Science Foundation.

The main problem was to avoid the charge of idiocy, for our endeavour was to represent a polite protest against the fundamental belief of every speculative thinker that the world can be consistently comprehended by aristotelian logic.

At first we hesitated. We did not know which presentation would be better, a philosophical or a mathematical one. Then Andrew quoted a letter from George Eliot to Miss Lewis where it was said that while mathematics is indubitable and immutable, and while no one doubts the properties of a triangle or a circle, doctrines infinitely important to man are buried in a charnel-heap of bones over which nothing is heard but the barks and growls of contention.

We decided that the layman is entirely wrong when he thinks that mathematical knowledge is more securely based than all other knowledge. Numbers do not exist objectively. They are self-referential mental constructs. This is what Alex told us.

There were very few, even among those with a classical bent, who failed to sense the exhilaration of listening to Alex, who for us was Godel the Second, the first being the famous logician from Princeton, whose work put an end to any attempt to reduce mathematics to mechanical handling. Even with honorary degrees, academy membership, and awards bestowed upon him, he began to display signs of depression, and died of malnutrition caused by mental disturbance.

What else than mental disturbance can follow a discussion like that when we asked the girl in the reference room to prepare a bibliography of all bibliographies in the library. She laughed and said that it would be reasonable to have that bibliography list itself. Alex laughed also and said that he wants a bibliography of all bibliographies that do not list themselves. The girl asked if that bibliography should list itself. Alex answered that if it doesn't, it should, but if it does it shouldn't. This was the final proof that mathematics is not reliable.

Even D.R. accepted our decision. He was one who consistently favored specific details over abstractions, no matter how many times he had been dismissed in some quarters, as a little too long on charm, and too short on substance, unengaged by big ideas, unless they could be broken down into parts.

Our thesis was that the methodology of science is currently reaching the frontier where the new skills of handling inexact concepts will become critical. Enduring vagueness is a method used by humans to reason about actions in a world perceived imperfectly. Using vagueness is the way humans perform for getting robustness into an unfriendly environment.

Now that we had the objective and a kind of ability to act and decide quickly, it was clear that a successful approach critically depended upon our presentation. We were not satisfied with the classical tone of the classical scientific reports. We decided to write a text with a powerful message, not perverted by the splendor of the schematization of the traditional scientific writing. We decided to write a new kind of text, where many topics can be discussed briefly and then dropped, only to be discussed again later. Not as a text, but as an essay; a loose presentation of ideas, like a good novel, exercising the daring perspicacity of the intelligent reader.

We started to write. We started with the obvious axiom that it is through man that vagueness comes into the world, because only he needs abstractions. When Dan asked what is it about the being of man that occasions abstraction, John Philiponus answered him, "Freedom to go upward to higher synthesis, looking for stable positions." When Dan asked why this craving for stable positions, John Philiponus answered him that stable means firm, fixed, not likely to move and to change. It seems men have a nostalgic, wistful longing for something they have known in the past, in a lost paradise where they were meant to stay unchangeable, like their creator.

Alex started to laugh, a sure sign that he was in a stable mood. For hours we debated why laughter is a natural tool to erase boundaries between precise predicates. John said that the mystic does the same thing using a methodology to transcend attributes. The ascetic attempts to wipe out his experience and attain a state of perfect neutrality.

Alex continued to laugh, and said that it is not easy to be an ascetic when the blonde goddess laughs in the reference room. Nobody noticed the remark. Andrew spoke at length about Max Delbruck, a Nobel Prize winner who was sure that infants are not born, as Kant imagined, with prior concepts of time, space, and the like, fully formed in their minds; they are born destined to acquire them as they mature.

We listened hungrily. The question for Delbruck was whether order is inherent in the world, and whether an adult's perception of it is the result of heightened observational powers, or whether it is simply a biologically useful illusion. In our opinion, it was an illusion. Such categories as time, number and causality may be serviceable within a limited domain, but they break down if we ask too much of them.

This was a starting point for a thorough examination of the mystic and his state of perfect neutrality. He has to develop new categories more fitting to perceive the world, and his apprehension of reality is more accurate. We concluded that the sequence in which various perceptions and concepts are acquired by them seems to be invariant, and the result is always the same: a world that does not obey the laws of Aristotelian logic.

This simple conclusion of course, influenced our report. If the experience of unity in contemplation results in the coinciding of opposites, then this is a dynamic process; a movement. This movement towards an ideal pattern takes place in the structure of concepts. Pulling back in this structure means to achieve equilibrium. This was the role of vagueness. Otherwise the transcendence cannot be explained.

As was usual, we started with the conclusion and used it as an introduction. First we said that transcendence signifies a trend towards totality, completeness and wholeness. To be sure we did not make a mistake, we went to the Advanced Oxford Dictionary of English and copied the definition. To transcend means "to go beyond or outside a description." Transcendence therefore, seeks a unification of a particular existence in such a way that every detail will be less emphasized, but still included. If we accept that transcendence discloses a constant openness in which man grasps freedom, then it is high time to obtain a deep insight into this natural phenomenon.

We did not have to worry because the report was building itself: everyone came up with his contribution, and dissipated even the dregs of confusion about the unity of our views.

We decided to start with examples. The first one was furnished by Andrew who selected a brand new theory of motivation. This was a theory elaborated by some scientists exhibiting authority. They preached for a long time that human needs may be organized in a hierarchy starting with basic requirements, and proceeding through a series of levels. No doubt about that: satisfaction is culturally defined. Andrew offered their idea of a structured whole consisting of a myriad of subconcepts, with the top being the good life, or something like that, and way down, the fact that we prefer steak because we might not sleep well if we ate the lobster.

In consequence, if one continues to pull back in the structure of sensual needs, the sophistication will grow up.

Here, John Philiponus mentioned Max the Confessor, who through his writings ranks with the eminent figures who belong to all mankind. Thirteen centuries have passed since he wrote about the knowledge tree from the Garden of Eden, which he said models the erection of the visible world, having both a spiritual meaning to feed the mind, and a natural power delighting the senses and perverting the mind.

Thirteen centuries before Max Delbruck, Max the Confessor said that Adam entered the world not with ready-made concepts; rather, he developed these concepts by interacting with the world. He had a choice how to develop these concepts.

Alex went again to the Oxford Advanced Dictionary of English and read loudly that perverse means "willfully continuing in wrongdoing; willfully choosing a wrong course contrary to reason." For many

days we labored over the definition of reason. Of course, at the beginning we asked all the wrong questions because we did not know the right ones to ask, and only later did we see how complete the Oxford Advanced Dictionary of English is when the definition (cause or justification for something) was translated as God's thinking by John.

Dan felt this was a striking illustration of the truth that Maximus wrote for all times, and that this was the reason that God forbade man's dealing with this poisonous tree, thus postponing man's acquisition of knowledge until he first consolidates his unchangeableness, thereby making adultery, fornication, and rape impossible, all which are born of temptation.

Andrew quoted Samuel Clemens, who took the pen name of Mark Twain, and said that Adam, in knowledge and experience, was in no way superior to a baby of two years of age. He had no idea of what the word death meant. He had never seen a dead thing. It is cruel to decree that all his descendents should be punished for the baby's trespass against a law of his nursery, fulminated against him before he was out of his diapers.

D.R. was more blunt. For him this tree of knowledge from the Garden of Eden was a usual vine, whose fruit is the usual grape, used for making the usual wine, a usual drug that changes the state of the body, blowing one's mind, causing extraordinary sensational sights in which time, space, object, number, and causality break down.

Dan did not like these trivialities, and tried to shift the discussion towards more serious topics. For him, Descartes provided the basis for the reality of scientific thinking. He was correct in saying that correct thinking proceeds from the premise that we possess no senses.

Pure thought, unconfused or distracted by the trivialities of the experiential world, becomes the sole source of reliable understanding: the coincidence of thinking and being. Newton's thought was consistent with the Cartesian duality of experience and reason, when the detached observer grasps the meaning and the relationship among events through an exercise of pure intellect. Finding the natural law is the competence of the human, and how deep we go with this finding is the performance of the finder. Einstein went deeper than Newton because Newton was prior to Einstein.

D.R. started to murmur that God made the earth and under the earth he put a small angel, and under the soles of the angel he placed an emerald rock, and under the rock he put a bull with one thousand big eyes, and under the bull came the fish Bahamut, and under the fish he put water, and under the water deep darkness, where men cannot see.

Bored by our daily pabulum of advertisement, gamesmanship, and innocuous position essays disguised as controversy, Dan began to hunger for real argument; for responsible conviction. He was aware that yesterday's outrageous and dangerous challenge often turns out to be today's status quo, that the most virulent accusation may one day be accepted as progress.

In many ways and for a long time D.R. was able to say no. Dissidents have their own rhetoric, one that can be studied in its full range of tones: resentful or resigned, angry or agonized, irate or ironic, varying in intensity and effect. He always wanted to say no, but in an elegant way. Educated in the artificial world of politics, able to be mild and polite, his dissent was not furious, but downright funny.

When we scheduled a debate on the existence of God for 7:30 on the evening of Wednesday the tenth of May, no one could have anticipated the phenomenal interest that would be generated. Shortly after seven the entire assembly had to be moved from the reference room in the old department of physics.

The featured participants were Dan and D.R. Dan took the affirmative position while D.R. defended the opposing view.

Dan began by outlining six arguments for the existence of God. An initial one was the nearly unanimous consent of mankind, in which atheists are viewed as elitist snobs.

The next items discussed were versions of cosmological argument. It should be taken that everything not self-sufficient depends on a cause.

Finally, he brought up the very transparent proof from design, which asserts that the regularity of natural processes cannot result from mere chance. Order implies a designer.

Then D.R. gave his presentation after some revealing remarks on what he called the context of the debate: the unprecedented worldwide religious revival that could not have been foreseen some years ago, when almost everyone thought that God was quite dead.

D.R. offered not discursive arguments against the existence of God. He simply asserted his belief that the universe has no built-in purpose, meaning or plan; meaning comes from what we give to the world. He also quoted Max Delbruck, who suggested that the real significance of quantum physics is that it forces us to view mind and matter as aspects of a unique system. The mind-matter dichotomy may enable us to order our experience more easily, but like our perception of time, space and causality, it may be an illusion. Matter is a mental invention, and mind a property of the physical world.

"Buddha," said Alex. His laugh, which started modestly, turned out to be an explosive bark, and we were sure that it grew from a sense of the misfortune of mankind which did not seek union with an infinite God. For this reason, it seemed strange that the moanings and the piteous short wrinkles of grief in Dan's forehead were accepted as justified through their expressive value; while laughter, as though it were some kind of slip or misdemeanor on the part of nature, was explained away. In laughter his face was moving, the mouth widened, the eyes sparkled and teared, the cheeks reddened, and the belly pulled in. This was the proof.

D.R. finished his segment with an attack against faith claiming that historically, belief in God was and is a prime force of hatred, destruction and bloodbaths. Conversely, adherents of the will to doubt have always been harmless.

He also quoted Mark Twain: "There are no peaceful nations now except those whose borders have not been invaded by gospels." During the past generations the poor have been taxed almost to the point of starvation to support the giant armaments which the states have built to protect themselves from the rest of the brotherhood.

This is the game which is so costly, ruinous, and silly. It is called statesmanship, but differs only from assmanship in its spelling.

Dan answered with Bruckner's "Le Sanglot de l'homme blanc," which he considered a coruscating critique of third worldism. For more than two hundred years, the western imagination has been captivated by the image of the noble savage, living undisturbed in a pristine Garden of Eden. What is more shocking than to find him set free from his oppressors, oppressing others in his turn; banana-republic Lenins ordering the extermination of millions, like crazed monsters who literally ate their opponents.

Everytime lesbians demonstrate for the right to adopt children, the herdsmen of Sudan are a little bit freer.

Everytime a guerilla shoots a soldier I am a little bit freer.

This was the sign—that in order to appreciate a cathedral, a perspective was required. Certainly, as we come closer to it, we shall have a better view of the statues, the portal, and the ornamentation; but we shall miss the general impression willed by the architect, which can only be obtained from a distance.

During the end of the spring, while trying to scrape our thinking and cut a path through the fabulous jungle of half-baked ideas, we discovered the department next door.

That department had studied for a long time the basic teachings of the great thinkers and had come up with the same problem. They were overwhelmed by impossible answers to impossible questions.

For instance, why is economics sometimes called the science of wealth, when it should be called the science of poorness? What is wealth, and what gives things value? As is turns out, things are valuable not because they are useful, but because they are scarce; not because they require labor to produce them, but because ethical principles influence the methods by which they are obtained. No doubt there has to be a reason explaining why a worker in Japan receives fifteen dollars per hour, and in Haiti only twelve cents. These became important, hot, unbelievable questions.

Dan was very excited and became very friendly with our new friends. He shouted with them, "down with oppression and coercion through science, deception, pseudo-convictions; churches of science becoming political parties; superstitions that say the historic process is controlled by immanent laws."

"Baloney," he shouted. And we laughed and shouted, "Baloney." Conceptions formed under the obvious influence of the shaky advances of natural sciences are nonsense. Imagine those thinkers who used science to predict new social orders, just as astronomers predict the return of the comet. To bring about the eclipse they organize revolutions. Ha! This was how we learned that in the past hundreds of years two questions always stood before mankind: where to seek the stones that are to destroy the old world, and what is the supreme authority to sanction the selection.

Old religions were inclined toward God. Modern religions are inclined toward science, although nobody today is able to answer why such extremes of power and fear exist in modern societies. We never found a scientific explanation for this troublesome phenomenon, and never stopped wondering why. Granted that the difference between rich and poor is as old as the world, poverty has never been quite so apparent as it is today, in the midst of such an abundance of material goods.

In the reference room, the girl was sure that Moses said go west. No doubt, mankind was put on earth for a purpose, and the maker sent along a book with instructions to reveal that purpose and to guide men.

But Adam rejected the guidance, stumbling in the darkness of his own murky science, answered D.R. She came up with three Bible quotations, arguing that wealth and power were promised to the children of God. Few have ever noticed this astonishing fact in the Scriptures. God began this world with one man to whom He communicated person-to-person. This man was able to choose enjoyable life and abundant well being; blessings caused only by a spiritual law.

But Adam listened to Satan and leaned on his science, answered D.R.

Not exactly, said the girl. One man, honest, upright, submissive, strong, purposeful, started an assembly of tribes, having as a birthright world power, vast material wealth, and resources.

Her extraordinary new explanation was based on the historical fact that ten of the tribes, invented by the strong and purposeful servant of God, were conquered temporarily by the servants of Devil, driven out of their land, and carried to the shores of the Black Sea. They never returned, as recently confirmed by Koestler in a book about their tracks. They disappeared along the blue Danube, a fact confirmed by Herbert W. Armstrong, who stated that some of them journeyed within the confines of the Thracian tribes, and later emigrated to Ireland, in the days of King David. He based this on the absolute evidence that "British" in Hebrew means "covenant man," and that all Irish annals speak of new settlers as "people of God."

We were fascinated by such accurate stories. Dan noticed our interest, pleasure, and excitement, and offered a new book published by Joseph Dragan of Milan, in which he described the movement of the Tracian tribes. In one illustration, he states that those who first landed on the North American shores came from the Valley of Danube.

He seemed to be right, because we had many other proofs that no matter what, why, and how, everything moves west; as for instance the sun, or the black death, the most devastating epidemic ever to strike Europe. Empires likewise move the same way.

He was right, because he was always right, a fact verified by us when we discovered he doubted the legitimacy of mathematics in economics, as was also expounded by Professor Nicholas Roegen in his wonderful book published by Harvard University Press. In it, he questioned the current store of economic ideas which do not explain why the dollar is weak when the president seems to be sick; a sign that belief, never quantified and never fully explained, is more powerful than all numbers.

He was right, because he discovered before us the ill-fated hoax of aristotelian logic. The difference between One and Many, with which Plato in particular struggled, has its roots in the fact that a quality does not necessarily pass from a concept to its concrete denotation.

No doubt that the best books are not the ones that give all the answers, but those that are full of provocative questions, examples, and inconclusive discussions. To those books you have to return again and again, and their inconclusiveness make them take a new aspect every time you return with a fresh background. They are always generous in giving staff to new thinking.

This was what happened when Dan discovered E. Barker, the translator of Aristotle's *Politics*. Answering why a new translation was necessary, he said that this is a book which is needed by the general reader of all the civilized world. It inspired the political thought of Thomas Aquinas, who in turn inspired Catholic Europe, which influenced Hooker, who drew from it the theory of governing by law, and consequently affected Locke, whose thought largely inspired the new world.

A famous saying reported by Boswell, is that the first Whig was the Devil. Lord Acton suggested an emendation: not the Devil, but Thomas Aquinas. Barker suggests Aristotle. He was the one to associate the scientist with the soldier, introducing the word cosmopolis, and justifying the kingdoms in Daniel's book.

The moment we saw this book, we were angry with him. If Aristotle was possessed by the devil, everything done has to be undone by the Angels of Light.

This is what Dan said. He was very excited. Andrew smiled and answered that as a joke, the idea is not bad. Alex liked the elegant line of reasoning. John considered the task very tough, requiring a special task force removed from evil empires and shorn of all passions. This would be a terrific experience worth trying, like the birth of a stone: hard, very hard.

He seemed to be thinking, and then confessed that some people in their unbelief, superstition and envy, will try to resist this approach. D.R. curled his lip and dismissed the suggestion with scorn.

★

There we were, going out very evening for a drink and a chat about the length of the legs of the beauties, with Alex the old gossip, telling us stories about hunting girls. John would tell us stories about mountain climbing, emphasizing the idea of being on an almost vertical slope, picking the way along a thin trail of steps chopped into the rock. This gesture of resplendence with defiance and whimsy was rewarded by the view from the top of the mountain; that magnificent view giving you that pride which all climbers know very well.

Of course we were asked about our intentions by friends and enemies alike. Dan often boasted to his neighbors about intelligent systems, a new generation of computers that will possess built-in reasoning power. They will learn, make decisions, and behave like men. No doubt you will stand before the machine the way our ancestors stood before the cereal crop: in reverence, pleasure, and awe. To be intelligent means to swallow the world, which at the beginning is outside, only to become at the end, a part of the soul.

D.R. always used to curl his thin lips and observe that in the reference room Dan is swallowing the blonde angel. He stands before the gorgeous goddess in reverence, pleasure and awe.

75

Alex, not mechanically inclined, always confessed that he was very confused about building machines. John remarked that after the fall, grace acts on man from outside. Dan's advice was that before building new machines, one has to understand the old ones. D.R. noticed that in the reference room, Dan was studying God's best machine. Dan answered him "Shut up you hussy" D.R. said, "Hey stone, don't be fresh."

Definitely, we were obsessed by the stone.

Of the many problems which exercised our minds from the beginning, none was so tempting as the pile of stones which becomes big if enough stones are added. This trivial observation ceases to be trivial when trying to answer a question like how many stones it would take to achieve this qualitative transformation.

Brain teasers like this expose the glaring and conspicuous lack of precision in language when drawing distinctions. Indeed, we seem to relish and derive pleasure from this looseness. There is nothing more natural than vague concepts. With a handful, we describe everything. The secret of vagueness exercised our curiosity for a long time. We spent more than two years sketching a theory, or something like that.

We did not know how to start. We did not want to quit the good path of applied mathematics for philosophical speculation. Only Alex grumbled that applied mathematics does not exist. We make wine, we drink wine, we make drinkable wine, but we do not make drunk wine: give me a break.

First, we were concerned with the question of the drinkable question exhibiting vagueness of application, because it is not clear just how drinkable a wine must be before it can be called drinkable. Then, we were concerned with the more important question of beauty. The existence of a plurality of distinguishable conditions of application does not in itself render the term vague. It seemed clear that a combination of features would be necessary, but there is no answer to this question.

D.R. assured us that the answer is in the reference room. No doubt about that: she is beautiful because she has beautiful legs. Surprisingly, Dan was also inclined to consider long legs as necessary, but Alex, a specialist, was sure that there are many beautiful women with short legs, God bless them.

As for claims that some set of features from the whole list is sufficient to make someone beautiful, they all turned out to be controversial. The task of removing the fresh elements of vagueness, which come to light with each new definition, seemed to be endless. The divide of quantification seemed to be insufficient. Nobody was able to swear that a beautiful woman may be defined as one who has a certain amount of long leggedness, although this was the case as illustrated by the goddess in the reference room: opulently, elegantly, divinely, breasted. Unbelievable, we damned fools, what is in a word.

Our main conclusion was that the collection of concepts, just because they are vague, has to be governed by nonaristotelian logic.

Unfortunately, knowledge is a very slippery concept, and the nonaristotelian logic seemed to be a very tangled affair. So we started to question the very meaning of knowledge, and landed in the field of cognition, which unfortunately again, is a very slippery concept. Since some distinguished cognitive models turned out to be very tangled affairs, we started investigations into the structure of concepts, which even if not a slippery concept, also turned out to be a tangled affair.

That summer was the deadline for submitting our report to the Science Foundation. Within ninety days of the expiration of an award, grantees were required to finish their report. This report was vital for getting new money for a new grant. Getting a new grant was considered an elevation to the peerage.

Dan noticed that the heart of science is in the theoretical structures by which experience gains a coherent explanation. Andrew answered that the so called facts of empirical observation are themselves theory-conditioned; damn it.

With a rasping voice, D.R. sneezed a derisive smile, sneered at our judgements, and scowled at poor Andrew. His suggestion was to begin with the biblical narrative. Dan answered that De Quincy was right. Of all the bores whom man in his folly hesitates to hang, and heaven in its mysterious wisdom suffers to propagate their species, the most insufferable is the teller of jokes. A nuisance that should be put down by cudgelling.

Much to our surprise, John said that the idea is not bad; this could be the way. He proposed we examine again the second law of thermo-dynamics; this was a sign that he was thinking about something.

The truth is that for quite some time he stopped trusting those aristotelians who overlook pioneering voices in favor of the trendy views of academic establishments. They exert a pressure to publish with less interest in content. When scholars seek university tenure, their work is often weighed for quantity.

The second law was perfectly clear. Everything is doomed to disorder. This was the aristotelian view. The nonaristotelians believed that Elohim introduces order periodically. There is no indefinite headlong drive toward disorder. It is as though some force in ratchet-like fashion catches the system just when chaos is imminent. John said it then propels it to a higher level. In so doing, the ratchet catches the system and boosts it to a new equilibrium. This is the meaning of the stone in Daniel's book.

Our work got a big boost when the quarrel between D.R. and Dan was at its peak, and our research was going to be doomed by disappointment and failure.

D.R. was sophisticated and ambiguous, and Dan did not like ambiguity. One day, he was listening to some ambiguous comments of D.R. regarding 2 Kings 23, where it is written that King Josiah took a grove out of the House of the Lord, burned it, ground it into bits and stamped it into powder. Only Dan knew that these groves were symbols of a goddess called Astarte. We did not understand what he was talking about.

D.R. said that those who worshipped Astarte practiced prostitution and roused themselves to spiritual frenzy through wild laughter. This last word made us cautious, but we still did not understand. We knew that D.R. is an expert in piquant squibs, so we listened attentively.

Not only did people bow down to the symbols of the Queen of Fertility, he continued, but they carried on a virtual orgy. That is why Josiah smashed the grove. He knew it was an abomination to Almighty God. We were devouring the story while Dan was being devoured by anxiety. The wild laughter was clear. D.R. was pointing to us, and Astarte was the goddess from the reference room.

As a climax to the evening's entertainment, D.R. concluded that many of the symbols were right here in the campus, in mute dedication to the great whore Astarte: obelisks, upright towers, and our male organs.

This was an unforgivable offense in the eyes of Dan and Alex as well as everyone else. We asked Dan to go skiing, and live alone for awhile. No ship could live in such a rough sea.

The Great Ski Chase was not a familiar event to most of the sports public, but that winter it was attracting thousands of participants. In those early days of the sport's popularity, the Great Chase attracted a few die-hard skiers who liked to push themselves to the limit. These days, when going for an aerobic high is in vogue, drawing a crowd of competitors that tests individual mettle is not difficult. Dan disappeared, and we continued to worry about the main idea of our report.

In that old room, in the old department of physics, after hours of exclamations, long awed silences, and many stops for laughing, none of us said a word when John suggested to rebut D.R. and reopen the problem of the grove.

Unexpected shyness came over D.R. but he tried to be patient. Then John surprised us. He said that the biblical narrative was useful. King Josiah had wiped out partial views, because he wanted to keep only the terminal view. Suffice it to say, in nostalgic retrospect, that D.R. was amazed and Alex started to laugh as never before. His facial distortions were proof that partial views keep man in ignorance. The biblical narrative worked again. More than that, it worked through D.R. The story was so funny that we were all in convulsions.

Back from the snow, the skier first did not believe John's attempts to link the volcanic upheavals in our research to King Josiah's groves.

Patiently, John answered him that the world is an incredible intricate web, so interconnected that no matter where you touch it, the response is felt in every other part of that web, in time.

Andrew added additional proof. He pointed out that it would be a mistake to think that cubism and the twentieth century revolution in physics were unrelated. When they erased old distinctions between figure and ground, stasis and mobility, plain space and plain time, they projected their soul.

We examined for hours questions. Why does the universe exist? Why did God create man, the origin of the sin and the role of the Tempter, the angel of darkness? An array of old and new problems was explored.

We concluded that adultery in the Garden of Eden between Satan and Eve had resulted in mankind's fall. That Cain was Lucifer's son, and that only Abel was the legitimate one. Instead of going along the path marked out for him by God, Cain turned aside. As a result, a new form of existence appeared on earth: that of partial views. By turning away, man put himself in a state that was contrary to his nature. Man's will is weakened by desire. But, and here was our point: Adam fell, but not from a great height of knowledge. The image of God is distorted by sin, but never destroyed. I can inherit Adam's corruption, but not his guilt. I can be guilty only if I imitate Adam. Period.

Only D.R. was stubborn. To him, we were a bunch of bananas in which hype had replaced fact, and faddism was synonymous with life. Others worry about freedom and food. We worry over whether or not we are guilty. The usual heavy stuff of the original sin. "Let me tell you something different, buddies. A real life story. My story. Not long ago, I got divorced. If I'd been married to her these past years, I'd be in an insane asylum right now. Or obese. Or anorexic. Or agoraphobic. Or brain dead. So, those people who are claiming perfection have to be chumps. There has to be degrees of perfection; a hierarchy of the saints."

He told us about his severe mental torment: how he sought professional help from a psychiatrist, and spent thousands of dollars on doctors; ranging from psychologists to hypnotherapists. They all walked away baffled, leaving him more depressed than before.

He told us how he met her a couple of years ago on the beach, where every man stopped dead in his tracks. Hearts skipped a beat and waves stalled in midair as this seraph of femininity and splendor, with light blonde hair, dark-tanned skin, and perfectly rounded breasts came strolling by. I was impressed by her itsy-bitsy string bikini. I noticed a ten year old boy dash out from behind a large rock. He was followed by a sight to behold: his sister was a knockout. She was then twenty-five years old, with a divine face, huge tits, and long shapely legs stemming out of the most gorgeous and roundest ass on the beach. We talked. She left with her brother trailing behind her. Then, the disaster. I married the angel, only to go to the devil. Even so, men who get divorced continue to get screwed. No politician dares to offend feminists. Statistics show that there are more women voters than men. No political party will entertain mens' rights policy in its national platform because no party is under pressure to do so. It is only a matter of time before an Eve will be put on the national ticket. Every major newspaper features advice columns for women by women. Eve is stronger than ever.

Only Dan answered him, "Nonsense! Before you throw up your hands in despair, let me say that you are wrong."

Dan was a passive resister. When he did not like certain laws, he did not want to break the heads of the law-givers. He simply did not submit, and hence suffered the penalties. He saw that there are always people ready to assert their power: to declare our thoughts illegal or immoral, to outlaw and declare obsolete our traditions, and to assert the authority to enforce their decrees. He was fascinated by the distinction between institutions existing by nature and those which exist by convention. He was convinced that a state is merely a conventional thing, that might or might not be, and only existed because some men agreed that it should. He objected to this on the grounds that it defeated natural rights, leading men to turn the state into a milch-cow, for dividends they never earned.

As a student he tried to dig into these philosophical matters, and liked Aristotle, who saw everywhere the growth of an initial potentiality into an end. But he was horrified when the blonde from the reference room opened his eyes with proofs that what Aristotle had in mind was the growth of the household into the village and of village into the state.

She seemed to be right, because in Genesis it is clearly written that God accepted the sacrifice offered by the shepherd Abel and rejected the sacrifice offered by the farmer Cain, probably because the shepherd is not related to villages growing fast into big states.

She was right, because in Genesis it is also written that Noah, after the flood, received the command to go out and to spread. They preferred to build cities, probably anticipating Aristotle's known definition of a citizen as one born of citizen parents. All this leads to the immorality of passports, borders, customs, and immigration services, accommodating the changing needs of those who turned the state into a milch-cow, and made it an association for the distribution of dividends never earned.

Only later he confessed his interest in the idea of a growing potentiality, whose end is the essential nature of everything, since man was made in the image and likeness of God. If so, man can move toward God.

A tremendous problem in itself, given the fact that all the paths to Him are guarded by serpents and griffins and other fabulous creatures, such as lionesses; opulently breasted, with elegant, breathtakingly shapes. They have no parallel except the black blonde goddess, invented by Brancusi, the sculptor, whose humor gently peels back the cover of man's weakness to the point where it is laughable, lovable, forgivable and redeemable. A barb at our knack of getting rid of our human frailties when they do not let us think.

This obliging, modest, nice man, who all his life was skeptical about women, was quite impressed by the blonde from the reference room. Dan considered that now it was high time to start a warm, strong family. The only reason to get married is to create offspring.

When he exposed this magnificent idea, which by the way seemed to be true, the goddess didn't say no because, we were certain she also thought it was true. But she said yes with a laugh, and the laughter grew, and we all joined in the laugh. As the noise covered everything for awhile, nobody knew what to say because everything was already said.

During the period of consolidation, when we tried to find a backbone for our report, Dan returned to his favorite theory of images based on the idea of likeness.

While the plans for explaining this idea went forward, we waited, without confessing so, for a translation into modern language acceptable to fellow mathematicians, noble critics, and peers.

Dan was also aware that these critics wait for occasions to prove their ability and find cracks in the flood of to-be-published papers, full of insignificant problems.

Since good Lord Kelvin, a first essential step in the direction of science was to find a practical method for measuring some quality. When you measure what you are speaking about, you know something about it.

Dan proved that a similar statement can be found in the writings of Leibnitz, who was certain that if we could find signs appropriate for expressing all our thoughts as exactly as geometry expresses the relationships of lines, we could extend this principle to all subjects that are amenable to reasoning. Thus, we would accomplish what is done in all mathematics.

It was impossible not to accept all these, first because they were true, and second because they did not contradict our model of knowledge, as presented in our first paper to be published in an outstanding journal devoted to the inter and transdisciplinary science of general systems.

This science has made tremendous advances in the last two decades, as evidenced in hundreds of books, various specialized journals, voluminous post-conference reports, and many established national and international societies. In this way, it reflected the course of the second industrial revolution, dominated by the computer, the beautiful machine designed to crunch numbers.

The journal sent our paper to a referee considered to be familiar with our research. The referee was astonished by the dazzling conclusion that science is not an outward push towards minute descriptions, but a pullback towards more vague synthesis. His observation was that such a view can lead to a pessimistic tendency to believe that knowledge is doomed to be nil.

We fought in defense of the paper, and argued that the growth of knowledge is not a cumulative process, but one of getting rid of the conflicts, as suggested also by Popper, a noted philosopher of science. He wrote many times that the task of science is to find a satisfactory and deeper layer of explanation. Although there are more and more paradigms, knowledge grows in the opposite direction, towards increased integration: towards unified theories, because the tree of knowledge springs from countless roots which grow up, rather than down, and tend to unite into one common stem. This growth is a purposeful process.

Obstinate, determined, difficult to deal with, the reviewer stubbornly continued to ban the publication of our bold paper.

Again, we answered with the phenomenology of the good philosopher Huserl, who wrote that image construction is a process heading somewhere. He also maintained that an image describes the tacit perimeter of a viewpoint, and the event of understanding is one in which a person opens himself up to new perimeters, thereby extending an old image to include a new one.

We insisted in vain on the fact that the opening of a new horizon gives brilliance to men just because they possess the wonderful mechanism of a pullback in the natural structure of concepts.

Definitely, something was profoundly wrong, and we decided to rewrite our paper. Carefully we examined the text, sentence by sentence. Our ignorance about new horizons which gives brilliance to men viewed as images of God and trying to improve their likeness to Him, seemed to destroy our credibility in the eyes of an informed reviewer. He suggested that we should peruse the most important twenty-five journals dealing with general systems published since 1944. We would see that the idea of an image is far from becoming a star.

In the last minute, John Philiponus came up with the brilliant idea of changing the two difficult words. Let us speak about competence and performance, terms in vogue in mathematical linguistics. They are accepted today at Stanford, Harvard, MIT and Yale. You know, they are more conformable to custom. Image and likeness sound strange, and only gave us trouble. In effect, the biblical narrative had to be kept secret. Not everybody liked it.

★

In that so sudden summer, Alex tried to cover as much ground as he was able. He devoted himself to the destruction of those prejudices which we had conceived to be our duty more than a year before. The idea of pleasure and pain were the first to be examined, and he undertook the evaluation of truth as the scientist's first task. Pleasures, particularly the delights of sophism, were naturally suspect.

He increased his readings with a savage and unfastidious appetite—books on history, eastern legends, everything related with the end of the world. The blonde librarian did not supply his needs with sufficient alacrity. Although refined, her theory was more or less the same: history dramatically validates prophecy and prophecy provides history written in advance.

He observed first that partial views are sterile sands where the blonde child wandered alone: bareheaded, barefoot, out of the patches of clarity and certainty. He did not say false reasoning intended to deceive, but he meant it.

She did not want to accept this suspicion. For her everything was quite simple: when Rome fell it seemed to be dead; prophecy shows that there is yet seven revivals. Napoleon represented the fifth

85

resurrection, Mussolini and Hitler tried again, but their resurrection, like the five that had gone before it, ultimately collapsed. He pursued some mental exercises which soon culminated in his own discovery of the seventh revival.

At this moment, the reading of Charles Higham's *American Swastika* turned out to be one of determining influence. This book of incredible depth, breadth, subtlety and wisdom contained endless layers of meaning; a first reading can only give hints of its richness. It had the odor of the jungle, too startling to be believed. Alex read long passages to the girl, emphasizing a long standing U.S.—S.U. connection.

She laughed, but he didn't. His facial expression was rigid, his manner of reading ponderous in the style of the Old Testament. There was something martyrish, resigned, and at the same time stubborn and accusing in his physignomy with its wide-open, fixated eyes and almost mask-like immobile features. When his reading was challenged, a pitiful, self-complacent smile played around the corners of his mouth, but soon faded away into his mask. When questioned, he answered from the start with a full repertoire of quotations. At first it seemed impossible to get him to speak his own opinion or to take a stand. The ideas of the book literally captured him, possessed him, obsessed him, and forced us into the same weird obsession.

The main idea was the most celebrated instance of a displaced person entering the U.S. after the war, Nicolae Malaxa, one of the wealthiest industrialists from Romania. He, along with Max Ausnit, became the financiers of the Legion of the Order of the Archangel.

At all brainstorming sessions there is a wielder of a bell, empowered to sound it at any manifestation of adverse judgements or laughings. This time we did not need him, as we were absorbed by the story and its details.

On January 16, 1941, at Berchtesgaden, Hitler was reminded of Soviet penetration in the Legion. On January 18, the chief of the Railway Transport in Romania, Major Doehring, was murdered. On January 22, street fighting broke out in the capital. Hitler was furious and ordered Von Killinger to flush out the rebels. Malaxa was held responsible, which led to his immediate trial. It was determined that he had supplied machine guns, revolvers and grenades, believed to come from American sources. General William Donovan was in Sofia that week and some German reports show that some meetings of the Legion were held in the American Embassy. A german Intelligence Officer, Otto von Bolschwing, who sheltered the rebellious leaders of the crushed Legion, was arrested by the Gestapo and taken to Vienna. After the war, he was cleared in the process of the denazification, and allowed to immigrate to the U.S. When the Russians took over Romania in 1944 Malaxa, accompanied by the Romanian Premier Groza, travelled to Moscow to seek permission to resume trade. On March 14, 1946, the U.S. Secretary of State Acheson confirmed that Stalin had approved the U.S. participation with Malaxa on a tripartite basis. Then, for some reason, Malaxa changed his mind, and fell away from loyalty to his partners. In 1951 he applied for permanent residence under the Displaced Persons Act, feeling sorry for General Marshall and his good friend Richard Nixon, who pressed for the introduction of a bill in that sense.

Some observations may be offered as to the various mechanical aspects of our brainstorming. Alex was looking for ideas. He announced the subject and delivered the background information. We offered a few suggestive pump-primers. Nothing else. These were so bandied about by Alex the Sweet, so juggled by Alex the Aware, so pawed and perverted by Alex the Great, that some distortions were to be expected.

At first, everyone celebrated them with awe and couldn't say enough in praise of them. When the praise was exhausted, we went to the other extreme. Finally we concluded that the U.S. itself is the seventh revival of the Roman Empire with two solid legs, the right conservative one, and the left liberal one.

Meanwhile, rival innovators like Andrew sprang up to claim that the new idea was not novel. (The almost universal testimony of those who have tried brainstorming is that it stands the pragmatic test. Through its employment individuals produce more ideas than they would otherwise. As brainstormers, we experienced side effects which made us happy. This element which Aristotle would have called catharsis, keeps any brainstorming moving.)

John noticed this danger. He mentioned Basil the Great in a text about prophets, and Denys the Areopagite in a text about Angels, and warned us about vain talk.

Andrew, who liked poetry and sophistication, came up with the teachings of Buddha, relating how soft zephyrs pass through the trees of a pure land outside the world of delusions. There, only the zephyrs stir the curtains of the pavilions and pass away in sweet music. Vain talk is music, this is what we said.

Even without exaggerating the importance of entering this last, rapid, and brief period of our story, we felt more mature in relation to all the dangers of sophistry, and tried to avoid the catharsis by a greater detachment and a more marked indifference to history which after all, is only a chain of partial views: treacherous, partial images; illusions of knowledge.

Even Alex became calm and aloof. He rarely paid visits to the reference room. Nothing, not even impious motivations in dark unknown nights, revived the brainstorming desire; the blonde image of Rome. With images banished, we switched seriously to the preparation of the report for the Science Foundation. The m ore mature we grew in experience, the more we recognized that the surest way to put together a text lied in the constant effort to reduce everything to the utmost simplicity; to strip our vines of all useless foliage, and to concentrate on what is important. Any other way of behaving is nothing but affectation. It soon shows itself in its true colors and becomes a mockery and a hindrance. This conclusion was likewise conveyed to us by centuries of experience, at least from the times of Saint Efrem of Syria, who summarized the meaning of "Lord have mercy upon me," by saying "Lord and Master, remove from me the spirit of sloth, of thirst for power, and of vain talk."

That summer, the press confirmed our conclusion, not in logical declarative language, but in a kind of prose poetry, similar to that of the Psalms: full of the singing of birds and the dancing of girls, perorations to will, joy, and eternity in thousands of colorful metaphors.

Every decent paper put on the first page man's space rendezvous with other crews, close enough to see into each other's cabin, trade gibes and inspect details. The astronauts could see Commander Lovell's beard and could tell that Colonel Borman was chewing gum. Later they flew ten times around the moon with Colonel Borman describing it as a vast lonely sight, not very inviting. Finally, Major Anders began reading the opening verses from the Book of Genesis, and so we learned that darkness was on the face of the deep.

Back on earth we found the black-and-white television pictures so sharp as to seem almost unreal. We expected the trip to be somewhat romantic. Borman's conclusion was a false assumption.

Alex told us about his divorce. He came home one night and she was gone. All she left was a note, "Dear Alex, fuck it." He cursed quietly, with the meaning that half the sorrow of the world is caused by making false assumptions.

Without exaggerating the importance of entering this period of our story, we felt more mature. We noticed a slight blurring of the outlines of people, places, and undertakings with which we were formerly so strongly attached; a more evident inclination to understand and sympathize, and a greater tranquility in judgements.

It was not the same in the winter when we were busy with the promotion of our results. Dan was very excited about selling a new theory of the names.

In the Garden of Eden, he said, the first act of the person called Adam was to give names to all cattle, and to the fowl of the air, and to every beast of the field, and whatsoever Adam called every creature that was the name. Names, from the very beginning were means for economy in human cognition. They were used to penetrate the unvarying patterns beneath the multiplicity of all real objects. Adam said apple for a large number of individual apples. He saw patterns of likeness and difference. No doubt it is only through these patterns of sameness that we see: the best proof that a consistent world exists out there and that we can find some accurate way of describing it.

Alex noticed that Adam was not astonished at the apparent failure of his attempts to use vague concepts for a precise description of nature. However painful his loss had been, he probably lost something that was very well worth losing.

Our final decision was that Dan should prepare the examples, and Alex prepare the mathematical framework. Everything was going to be assembled by John, in an attempt to emphasize his new syllogistic reasoning scheme in a categorial framework. With a curled lip, D.R. was categorical, "Don't tell me that there were such things in the Garden of Eden."

When the paper was ready we held a meeting to read it.

D.R.'s comments were couched in cold terms, a kind of opposition disguised in the framework of pragmatic romanticism. He believed that the value of our research depended only upon its practical bearings. On the other hand, his approach was marked by feeling, rather than by intellect. He preferred grandeur to proportion.

In another paper published that year, he claimed a most ambitious research effort leading to a theory of models. It celebrated a new way of thinking that holds complexity; for example, beauty is as much a property of the beholder as of the object being observed. The trouble with system theorists, D.R. contended, is that their failures are attributable to the fallacy of regarding complexity as a system property: an attitude originating in the Cartesian mind-matter duality and its consequent philosophy of reductionism.

In his later years it appears D.R. had come to recognize that considerable leverage for his cause might be gained from alliance with us. Despite D.R.'s presumptiousness, we enlisted behind him, because we too were concerned with ill-defined systems. But we did not love each other. A loveless marriage, one could say.

Nobody knew anything about him. Only Andrew was able to find out that D.R. had had a quizzical love for his mother, a pure hatred for his father and a cool selective response to his maternal grandmother. Although he lived with her on and off, he did not cry when she died. His mother introduced him to music, the libraries, and the joy of reading. Because he was a superior student, with excellent grades, his classmates slapped, stoned or snowballed him. But he loved school. He owed his success to the good upbringing his parents had given him. As a student, he discovered that he could put words together to make what seemed to him, magic. It was said that he was not vulnerable to insult, but we saw enough of him in subsequent years to observe that when subjected to offensive and icy treatment by the blonde goddess, he was capable of jagged anger and vengeance, instant or retroactive. Otherwise, he was patient and very interested in John's knowledge, particularly about the angels created before the Garden of Eden. To him, they served a hierarchial structure of procedures and functions, allowing God to easily modularize his programs. Adam came later, being a little lower than the angels. (Though we humans have the awesome potential of becoming far greater.)

D.R. went so far as to ask John about the rebellion of the Archangel Lucifer, that brilliant morning star. We were dumbfounded because he did so without curling the lip. John did not seem to be very surprised and answered that this superb creature with supreme power and beauty was perfect: state-driven rather than hard-coded. No doubt about that. Satan is a knowledge-based system writing his own program.

In spite of interminable discussions, we sent out the paper. The journal appointed D.R. as one of the referees. He answered that sometimes he was finding himself reading the text in a fruitless attempt to answer two questions. What was this paper all about, and what was it for? Serenely, he wrote that no one would be able to comprehend what the authors were talking about.

Menaced by this event, we feared the possibility of finding ourselves at the crossroads with blinders on, at a time when choosing which road to take may determine our whole future. We decided to organize a seminar and invite people.

Dan was hundred percent in favor of this. Andrew was very excited. Alex was cheerful. John, skeptical about the outside world, cool and aloof, started a story about a rich man in hell and a beggar called Lazarus, carried by angels to patriarch Abraham's bosom. He wanted to dip the tip of his finger in water and cool the rich man's tongue, an impossible act due to the great gulf between heaven and hell.

But we said that times are different now. So we sent invitations two months in advance. Many confirmed their acceptance. We coordinated the tactics. Dan would emphasize the practical aspects, while John would nail down the principles. Alex would give the mathematical framework. The seminar took place at the end of the winter.

It was like entering the atmosphere of hell because their chirping made us nervous. Before we started our prepared presentation, John made a few remarks about demons. He explained that being immortal, they don't die. Punishment for them is not death, but an eternal thirst for their source. Nobody cared because we were obsessed by the formidable task of convincing them about the soundess and the potential future of our research.

Then we started the battle. We told them that the real task of artificial intelligence is to repudiate the technological imperative of precision. No pedestrian put-in-the-equation-and-turn-the-crank program will shed any useful light on such matters. The main problem is to reduce the world to manageable proportions. We invoked Tocqueville, who declared the importance of establishing a perspective.

We used his example of a traveller who has just left a vast city and climbs the neighboring hills. This was John's favorite example because he kept saying that God loved the shepherd Abel. Shepherds don't like cities. They move, and in moving they achieve something extraordinary, a synthesis of the world.

Our version was shorter. We didn't say shepherd. We said traveller. As the traveller goes further off he loses sight of the men he just left, and their dwellings are confused into a dense mass. He can no longer distinguish public squares, and he scarcely traces out great thoroughfares. His eyes, however, have less difficulty in following the boundaries of the city. He sees the shape of the whole. The details of the immense picture are lost in the shade, but he conceives a clear idea of the entire subject.

With this example we wanted to show that one key to complete understanding is the pullback to a point where the whole can be fully embraced. At this point one will make less detailed but more sure remarks. Here the perceived objects will be less distinct but the principal facts will be more certain.

After this example we switched to another idea. We said that concepts are views. We illustrated this idea with a second example, that of several blind men asked to describe an elephant in the dark. One touched his legs and described the animal as being a pillar. Another touched his ear and described the animal as a fan. A third touched his trunk and described it as a pipe.

With this example, we wanted to show that views provide a simple but efficient measure of hiding the world from seers who are not authorized to access the truth. The principal purpose of views is to simplify the perception, with the advantage that different seers can see the same reality in different ways.

This was Dan's favorite example because he kept saying that God did not love Cain because he was greedy and stood before the cereal crop in reverence, pleasure and awe. He didn't move; he saw only one reality, that of his stomach.

We finished with the evident conclusion that any paradoxical statement which contradicts a previous one is the result of a partial view, which of course can be enlarged by combining it with other different views. Here we stressed, with a wealth of mathematical methods, the beauty of the structure of concepts.

Analogy gives credibility. We quoted Godel and suggested that undecidability generated by conflict can be avoided by pullback to higher levels of vagueness. This is the dimension of knowledge, the human dimension. There is no doubt, infinity is faced by men through vagueness.

Following this short presentation, we answered a tremendous number of questions. A friend of ours who slept all the time, concluded that our research was on the right track. Another fellow, somewhere between us and the provost, said that each generation attempts to describe human nature in relevant terms as embodied soul temporarily existing in a transitory physical world. Today, in nontheological terms: either naturalistically as an animal, or culturally as a machine. New technologies change our perceptions. This made him proud of mankind. We can split the atom and walk on the moon, we have the computer, and we have breathed life into a finger-sized slice of pure sand.

Finally, we saw D.R. whispering something into the ear of the

Dean, something like: Who the hell do they think they are, how do they dare to fool us, and other similar evaluations.

He barely got sufficient control of himself when we met him in the cafeteria. We didn't say anything because resentment is the most toxic of drugs. Neither the provost nor the Dean said anything. We understood that most people are neither for us nor against us, they were busy thinking about themselves.

We decided to go further and present our results at a congress on cybernetics and systems, which, that year, was supposed to be held under the banner of ill-defined systems. We decided to present our paper to the big holy names who had the power of life and death, being entitled to endorse our ideas to give us the necessary prestige. Oh, the sweet smell of it!

In the middle of summer, all the big names were there, either as speakers or hidden in enigmatic fringe meetings ending with copious dinners, as specified by the Science Foundation which carefully takes care of its children. This is the mother of all those whose names are known from their papers, written by their graduate students happy to be in good schools.

Everybody was making a parade of his knowledge. We saw them in the majestic lobby of Sheraton, in the imperial ballroom of Mariott, and in the unbelievable Hilton, where we felt as though we were entering the atmosphere of ecumenical councils and they were like high pontiffs. Their warbling made us a little bit nervous. The world of science was bubbling over with joy, high spirits and laughter: long live the Science Foundation.

The living, physical beauty of a congress full of young beauties seemed to be overwhelming. As one marvelously formed performer moved, another was coming into view. Their deportment is proud and graceful, almost an idealization of deportment. The women are dignified. Their hips do not waggle when they walk. Their bearing indicates self-awareness in the best sense of knowing who they are. No pitying smiles, no silent reproaches, nothing at all.

In our section, we were supposed to speak last in a row of five speakers, ordained according to their importance.

The first one was greatly applauded because his message of hope was that human cognition is like machine computation.

The second one was convinced that an essential property of an ill-defined system is that it lends itself to no simple analysis. His conclusion was that, if we want to understand them, we have to analyse their observers.

The following speaker was a young man from Brazil. He proved that a population dispersed over an immense country, with cities as points of contacts, is incapable of formulating its interest, for in each region it is conceived differently from a different viewpoint. It is true revolutions do happen, but they lead to a re-division of wealth, after which history begins all over with a new aristocracy, new usury, and new uprisings begun by smart, self-declared prophets who hunt for more power.

Here John Philiponus had a short intervention. He noticed that a population of shepherds doesn't have this disadvantage. Shepherds move, and in moving, they achieve something extraordinary: a model of the world. No smart self-declared prophet can fool them. They don't need revolutions. Believe it or not, the word revolution has had from its beginning a primary astronomical sense referring to the regular circuits of heavenly bodies. Being under an open sky, the shepherd doesn't believe in whirlings, turnings, great change of affairs, or smart prophets.

The fourth speaker was of a different breed. The message was that the prophetic process can be viewed as a counterpart of a biological evolution. Individuals depend on groups, which depend on cultures, that depend through prophetic processes on individuals and their views. A prophet is a spokesman of a view.

The speaker was determined, confident, and sure. A capricorn woman with perfect proportions, magnificent breasts, and an impeccable skin. She reminded us of the goddess from the reference room who all of us worshipped.

Finally the chairman invited us to make a brief presentation because our paper seemed to be a little bit out of the stream. We produced a short abstract, emphasizing that by using linguistic descriptions, we escape being involved in uncertain statements. We had confidence in the truth of vague concepts just because they are vague. The vaguer the concept, the stronger our confidence. The example was the concept of God, the supreme view.

Our forte was the second part of the communication in which we tried to explain the relationship between knowledge and views. The thesis was that man, although not infinite, is attracted by infinity. Instead of gravitating toward it, some try to become one with it by absorbing a large number of views. The result is a fall into an accentuated state of blindness. Thus, by their irrationality, by their deceiving character, by diverting man from his goal; views keep man in the darkness of ignorance. The conclusion was short and devoid of views.

This formulation was due to Alex, but we did not mention here the example of Godel, whose work put an end to all the attempts of understanding the world by separate views. Even with honorary degrees bestowed upon him, Godel began to display signs of depression, and died of malnutrition caused by mental disturbance.

There were no questions nor comments and we left a little bit dissapointed. On the way out, we read an announcement that a reception would be held the next day. There, the mayor gave us pink champagne and a speech about science and its role in a very scared world.

It was only when the blonde goddess came to us smiling, oh the sweet smell of that smile, that we had a good time, and a thorough discussion about prophets, scientists and all those detached from everything the world so highly strives after; honors, praises, temporal comfort, affection, pink champagne and all kinds of things, narrowing the overall view.

It was Alex the Sweet who observed that Diana, the goddess of the hunt, wouldn't have looked better than our blonde goddess. Dan made the wise remark that it is not so easy to renounce the world in some circumstances; to turn your heart the moment you perceive some sensible weakness. Andrew didn't say anything.

The plump marvel with glossy blonde hair, light to lift yet weighty and slithering in the hand, with a hint of swarthiness in the flesh, and a trace of smut beneath that translucent skin, smiled and said that total detachment does not consist only in being detached from the world, but it obliges the soul to be in a certain sense, detached even from God; which she murmured with sweet and maiden bemusement, something like a poem.

Alex the Aware said that one must be detached from desires to be delivered from the prison of the body. In this way, one can feel God and be united with His view, without interruption.

We were struck by the way she held her chin, her pat nose, her slim arms, and her delicate shoulders. Dan said that as God allows you to feel the sweetness of His blessing, you must be careful not to become attached by this consolation.

We laughed, and she laughed, and Alex the Great declared that although we must exert all our energy into trying to conquer our passions, we must nevertheless work at this without being carried away by the zeal.

She laughed, and we laughed. She was so abundantly and so lavishly endowed, and we were so bewitched, that John Philiponus's conclusion nearly went unnoticed. In it he determined that you must trust to love your own abjection, remaining satisfied with what view it pleases God to give you, having confidence that the Almighty in his goodness, will give you what you need to serve Him.

★

Over July, the chapters of our report to the Science Foundation were more or less sketched. In August we only had to decide on a short explanatory introduction.

After not too many debates, we concluded that the backbone of this introduction had to be a history of nonaristotelian logic.

We were aware that in order to meet the needs of the Science Foundation, our account could not be based on the assumption of any previous historical reader knowledge.

What we wanted was a coherent analysis of sources. This meant that it had to start at the beginning, with the origin of the nonaristotelians. It must introduce every name or event that was an integral part in the account. All others had to be ruthlessly deleted, no matter how firmly imbedded in historical protocol.

Asked for help, the reference room answered with ambiguous answers. We were told that great obscurity hangs over the period of transitions which immediately preceded the nonaristotelians. It was as though the first century was shrouded in a mysterious darkness.

We turned back to our internal resources. We remembered that John Philiponus could go completely out on historical research, spellbound with facts. History was his life. His vast knowledge of it always left us dumbfounded. He was destined to dig and come up with a fluent and complete history of nonaristotelian logic.

John spent a long time just roaming around, learning and looking. He had an uncanny perception and a fine sensitivity. With intuitive power, with a faraway look in the eyes, as if they contained a mysterious knowledge that could not be penetrated, he was always analyzing and asking point-blank questions. Gathering the waters of knowledge and pouring them out again was his role. His ability to plunge into the unknown and absorb its secrets, yielded ideas which were often considered strange, but that was just because his critics were not tuned decades ahead as he was.

Even when we tried to structure our ideas, and Alex came up with mathematical definitions, John Philiponus was the one to attract the attention that there is nothing new under the sun.

He started with a presentation of the predicates that are suited for Godhead. For this purpose, he said, the predicates that are most valuable for men can be attributed in the superlative to God. Thus, if men are good, then God is best. If men are potent, then God is omnipotent, and so on, until everybody will notice the big distance; the deep abyss between creatures and creator. The fact is that the predicates are rather misleading and decrease the sublimity of the essence of God.

Therefore, if one says about men that they are good, it is more proper to say about God that He is not good. Further, if one preaches about men that they are potent, then it would be more suitable to say that God is not potent. This is the origin of nonaristotelian thinking which, although it has a disturbing and close to heresy character, nevertheless was adopted by the most Faithful Fathers, and can be found in the writings of nearly all authors of the Middle Age.

There were very few, even among those with a mathematical bent, who escaped the sense of exhilaration when working with John. For us, he was Erigena Scotus Johannes the Second, who didn't always keep himself on the right path of the faith, but nevertheless died happy in his bed. Alex begged John to continue.

However painful their loss was, he added, by losing the predicates the Fathers probably lost something that was very well worth losing. Negation does not give existence. It indicates only a lack or a loss. No view is safer than a false view. We must not be too astonished at the apparent failure of our attempts to use concepts for any description. Those who did not follow this path have littered the intellectual and philosophical graveyards with corpses of their failed efforts.

There, in the old department of physics, his voice was swathed in velvet. There was more effort in the top notes, but happily more of a sense of dramatic commitment as well. A certain reserve still kept him from lashing out. Sometimes his voice offered not only a glow that seemed to hover in the air, but had an occasional sharp edge that helped give his face dramatic depth and range.

The most amazing mistake, he continued, was made by Aristotle and Plotin, who considered that the Absolute One does not think, because thinking is not perfection. According to aristotelian logic, in order to think, the subject has to have an object in mind. Therefore, if the Supreme One would think, it would stop being One.

Now, if God thinks, thinking is real existence. By thinking himself, the Father does not become two in being, and knows himself both as thinker and as the one who is thought. He beholds His thought and, simultaneously, knows himself as the source of this image.

It was with him, in that room, that we learned about all those who succeeded in understanding that aristotelian logic is dangerous, leading to false paths. We were all mesmerized by their knowledge, although we found out that in the Eastern Roman Empire there were no creeds in the modern western use of the word; no normative summaries of what must be believed.

We asked him, where did you find all these sources, and he confessed that his sources were from the Valley of Danube which had been affected in an indirect way by the huge cultural upheaval which transformed western Europe.

That time D.R. laughed three times. First when John mention the Valley of Danube. Second, when he explained again why God thinks. And third, when he understood him. We asked ourselves what could be the reason that some people laugh and others do not. We went to the library, asked for help and received the ambiguous answer that there is a Treaty of Laughter. We looked and found three definitions.

Isaac the Jew, who was very celebrated among the Arab doctors of his time, was the first of all those who have attempted to define the nature of laughter. For him it was a trembling and a noise made by the chest. This was initiated by the movement of the soul when that which is introduced by joy falls upon the mind.

Later, Gabriel de Tarroga said that laughter is a sound-producing movement of the spirit, accomplished by contortions of the facial parts for having obtained joy and delight.

Finally, Gil Fracastoro, most learned philosopher and doctor, defines it as a movement composed of wonder and joy; which is why there are contrary forces in laughter. For wonder holds the mind somewhat in suspense, while joy expands it.

We accepted all explanations. Joy fell upon D.R.'s mind and the contorted parts of his face. The other parts were held by a terrible wonder; something unusual, and inexplicable. He looked at us in open-mouthed bewilderment.

Uncontrolled fires, unfortunately for their victims, not only grow but do so at a profoundly uneven pace. An incipient fire expands more or less steadily up to a point, after which there is a catastrophic event called flashover. This is what happened to D.R. He became interested in the history of the nonaristotelians.

He requested more facts: documents accepted by scholars, preferably neutral observers. John came up with the *History of the Decline and Fall of the Roman Empire*, whose last expansion was at the expense of the Dacians. Gibbon, the author, stated that these most warlike people dwelt beyond the Danube, and that they insulted with impunity the majesty of Rome. The barbarians believed in one God; their idea was that you cannot have peace without armies, nor armies without pay, nor pay without taxes.

In a book by MacKendrick, published by the University of North Carolina, John discovered the meaning of that insult. In Nero's reign, the Roman governor of Moesia was named Plautinus Silvanus, about whom one knows a good deal from an inscription found in his family mausoleum near Tivoli, fifty miles east of Rome.

The inscription records that he transplanted more than one hundred thousand transdanubians with their wives, children, and chiefs. Kings, hitherto unknown to the Roman administration were forced to pay taxes.

"Taxes without representation," murmured D.R., in an ecstasy of delight. "Quite so," answered John. "Roman schoolboys brought up on tales of heroic military actions taken against the inferior and barbaric Dacians: treacherous natives who were greatly influenced by a resolute bearing. "Quite so," answered John. "Cruelty and bloodshed forgotten in the praise given to brave soldiers who administered justice to vast populations in remote provinces, bearing the civilized man's burden, to paraphrase the great Kipling. "Quite so," confirmed John, and continued.

So, to the strength, fierceness, and contempt for life, the Dacians added the nonaristotelian idea that God thinks, and by thinking himself, the Father does not become two in being. To be nonaristotelian was a charge of malice and infidelity. Under the reign of Trajan, the tribe of nonaristotelians were sought out and punished. Outrages and suffering followed.

As a romanticist, D.R. had the quality of allowing full play to the imagination. He imagined bodies being torn to pieces by claws, women tied by one foot and raised on high through the air, head downward, with their bodies completely naked and without even a covering; furnishing a shameful, cruel, and inhuman sight to all the onlookers. Such were the happenings. "Probably," said John, and continued.

Hadrian succeeded to the sovereignty. To him, Aristides addressed a treatise as a defense, as noticed in 1878 by the Mecharite monks of San Lazzaro, at Venice. They published a Latin translation of an Armenian fragment together with a homily under the title "Two Sermons of Aristide, a Philosopher of Athens." In 1880, Harris of Cambridge discovered a Syrian version in the convent of St. Catherine on Mount Sinai, and translated it into English.

John's voice continued to be swathed in velvet, but there was no more effort in the top notes. No reserve kept him from lashing out at ancient history. He soon found himself at a loss to determine by what rule of justice he should direct his conduct. He had no more desire to continue, as if to do so would have hurt him.

He felt they had learned their lesson. They knew that any Augustus disguised in any form of commonwealth, no matter how humbly he professed himself to a broadminded senate, is a wolf trying to eat the mild sheep. They never trusted the emperors and their legions. Protected by very cold winters, in the summers they expected to move up into the mountains with their flocks. They were shepherds, the children of Abel. They survived many imperial systems which promised to restore the innocence and fertility of the golden ages only to disappear in failure. All the heresies which denied that Reason was with God from the very beginning, or was a dependent and spontaneous production created from nothing by the will of the Father, had a finite duration. Legions of missionaries were sent to explain to them how erroneous were their beliefs which kept them in their barbaric harmony with the mountains.

D.R., as a romanticist, exercised his quality of allowing full play to his imagination. He was sure that the shepherds did not know how the scholars first believed in the meter engraved on a platinum bar between two fine scratch marks, and later in the wavelength of light measured in a vacuum during a fraction of time; geared not to everyday life on earth, but to the abstruse dictates of Einstein's physics.

D.R. paused. John didn't say anything. We imagined the mountains, the sheep, the shepherds gazing over space and over time; skeptical, doubting the truth of so many claims and so many theories which boiled in the flatland, until violent revolutions erupted, unleashing strange forces which were supposed to build a new world. A Garden of Eden with its pastoral life was no longer suited to the advance state of the flatland.

For hours we discussed how the happiness and the glory of a technological reign were promised by proud aristotelians, and how the nonaristotelians were considered underdeveloped. A dreadful conclusion, because we imagined how many opportunities remain for those who wish to do them harm in the disguise of a development program based on the ancient idea that you cannot have peace without armies, nor armies without pay, nor pay without debt.

D.R., the romanticist, with full play of imagination, imagined outrages and suffering: the fingers of both hands pierced by sharp reeds under the tips of the nails, and other sufferings that are shameful and inhuman; as for instance no heat in the winter, and long lines for food.

John stopped him. He judged himself the adequate appreciator of his own people, and he judged the Dacians the most wonderful people in the world. He wanted to record their strengths, their resiliency, courage, and humor, not their sufferings which the aristotelians devised with more than ordinary eagerness: displaying their cruelty as a kind of wise virtue, always striving to surpass one another with their more recently invented torture called debt, as if prizes in a contest were involved.

Slowly our discussion shifted into the murky topic of international debt. Dan outlined literally dozens of strategies for getting through the Third World debt crisis. The arithmetic of debt means that some nations could do better in default, he argued. Most of the plans failed to provide carrots to match the sticks.

With a sardonic smile, D.R. whistled something about how the debt was used to finance cronies, Tiffany jewelry, and a lot of pollution. No doubt about it: these bankers must have known; they must have been really stupid or they had malicious intent. Whether through stupidity or cupidity, they are guilty.

It was the same as saying that social engineering is an extension of the technological imperative, which, during the past several centuries, has sharply separated man from, and fostered the ruthless exploitation of, nature.

No one knew for sure what was his message. In D.R.'s view, the real task before man was to repudiate the technological imperative; to rejoin the community of life and to renounce our drive for sovereignty over everything that lives. But we did not understand what he meant by all these texts, until Alex told us what he learned from Andrew.

In the sixties, while studying economics at Berkeley, D.R. had served as a varsity cheerleader and class president. Later, something turned his considerable talents leftward.

Dan tried to calm him down by pointing out that countries have
defaulted for hundreds of years, and memories are so short. In a
decade, they get back their credit. But there are threats that have
meaning: their exports will be embargoed, their assets frozen, and
their nose cut off.

D.R. expressed scorn by sneering. He curled his lip to bare the
canines. He said something about a forced overthrow or replacement
of an agreement by those subject to it. No doubt about it.

John Philiponus had doubts. First, the empires are restless
organisms constantly renewing themselves. They change their
names into superpowers and work together to survive in a highly
centralized world. Second, the shepherds learned by experience to
take the bad with the good. For them the word revolution has
absolutely no meaning. The word was invented by Cain.

"Don't tell me," said D.R., "that in all these centuries your
shepherds didn't try to jump outside their wonderful mountains."
John Philiponus acknowledged that there were adventurous shepherds
who sometimes made the mistake of quitting their mountain.
Everytime they were punished with deception, even when they
entered high office. "Aha," curled the lip of D.R. John gave an
example. Justin, who as told to us by Gibbon, deserted the more
useful employment of shepherd for the profession of arms.

On foot, with a knapsack, he followed the high road of the Capitol
Hill of that time, gradually obtained the rank of general, senator,
and finally president. We imagined Constantinople, the principal
cockpit in which Justin struggled for dominance at the start of the
post-aristotelian era in Roman politics.

It is true that Justin had never been instructed in the knowledge
of the alphabet, but his nephew Petrus Sabatius, whom his uncle
had drawn from the rustic solitude of Dacia, was educated. Gibbon
is very precise in the description of what happened. Presidential
hopefuls in both parties faced a primary election early enough,
perhaps, to have a major impact on the nominating conventions.
The standard-bearers chosen at the conventions found themselves
competing furiously, such that another candidate for the purple was
stoned.

As a president, Petrus Sabatius was culturally inclined. He built a temple of eternal wisdom which remains after centuries as a monument to his fame. He was a lover, a conqueror, and a lawgiver. He espoused programs designed to appeal to the region's patriotism, fiscal conservatism and dynamism. It is not clear how he succeeded. It is clear that the country was changing, that the change meant a partisan realignment. Many patricians underwent the ceremony of baptism, and labored, by their extraordinary zeal, to erase the suspicion of aristotelianism.

The perplexing crosscurrents of his administration can be seen more vividly if one takes into account his wife Theodora. Gibbon states that her vices were not incompatible with devotion. She was a beautiful woman, long-legged, opulently breasted, with wonderful skin.

D.R. wanted all kind of details, and the presentation shifted again towards beauty: her beauty, her venal charms, her pleasures; and how a prostitute came to be adored as a queen by magistrates, bishops, and victorious generals. D.R. was convinced that beauty was her secret. Alex bet on her guts. Dan did not know what to say, but wanted to know what happened with the aristotelian logic. John furnished us with the details.

Petrus Sabatius suppressed the schools of Athens which had degenerated from their primitive glory. This is what Gibbon asserts and he did not have any reason not to trust him. John Philiponus was spellbound with facts.

The sagacious minds of the aristotelians extravagantly explored the deepest questions of science, denying the limitations that biology has set on our understanding of the world. Over the centuries, they have progressed from being able to make descriptions, to being able to prove that it is impossible to make such descriptions. According to their logic these two contradictory theses cannot coexist.

Instead of committing suicide, they embraced the resolution of seeking in a foreign land the freedom to believe that the underlying nature of the world is inconsistent. They heard and credulously believed, that the republic of Plato was realized overseas. They were soon astonished by the natural discovery that this republic resembled other countries of the globe, in that bigotry and a spirit of intolerance prevailed.

Of course, when everybody understood the power of inaccurate descriptions, the department of physics received new buildings and funds for more research. This left us alone in the old building close to the library; a donation from the lovers of science, a memorial to those patrons who believed that the world is not intrinsically resistant to a meaningful description. Petrus Sabatius was certainly pragmatic. John Philiponus told us how he opened the imperial eyes against the aristotelian notion that the stars must be the eternal rotors of that eternal motion we call the natural process.

And we laughed for hours, because everything laughable is a nonaristotelian syllogism with two premises: one undisputed and one unexpected. Only D.R. did not laugh. He wanted to know what happened to the shepherds and why they disappeared from the stage for a couple of centuries. John seemed reluctant to join him again.

They knew that controversy about the irrationality of describing the world which is the offspring of folly, that silence is preferable to arrogance, that man, ignorant of his own nature, should not presume to scrutinize history.

Therefore, they polished their carols. This was his answer.

We switched to the carols. "What carols?" asked D.R. "Songs of joy," answered John, "songs to bless the year: the coming in, the going out, the rest, the travelling about, the rough, the smooth, the bright, and the drear." But this was invented in England. Not exactly, and we heard how three shepherds were united. "Oh Heaven's Sunlight, Golden Floral Sunlight," and thus inspired, they decided, "Come ye all together, dainty flowers we must gather to create a wreath divine, with gcod will to be entwined, for the Lord." He sang the better to understand, with more effort in the top notes. A certain reserve still kept him from lashing out. His voice offered not only a glow that seemed to hover in the air, but an occasional sharp edge that helped give his face dramatic depth.

When he stopped, the depth disappeared. His voice offered no more glow and his remarks were marked by rhythm.

Their perfection was accomplished not in abstraction but in the trivia that made up their days. They did not dream of the big break, the great conversion, the moment to change all moments.

Without effort, with his usual voice swathed in velvet, he drew the conclusion.

They knew that God is not nature. But however remote from them in His essence, in His energies, God revealed Himself to them. They knew that these energies were not something that exists apart from God, not a gift which God conferred upon them.

Rather, they were God Himself in His action. For His essence remained unapproachable, but His energies came down to them. Their nonaristotelian logic told them that God is known and unknown, in the same time, and that man is heart and mind, in the same time. In the divine energies, they were not overwhelmed by some vague concept, they were brought face to face with a person. They never knew what scholastics is, what it is to turn God into an abstract idea, a remote and impersonal being whose existence has to be proved by metaphysical arguments. They didn't know anything about technological somnabulism, because they were not the victims of any sleepwalking through our technological world, which believes that technical gadgets are possibly linked to human well-being. They were pure. And they still are. Some of them: those who didn't come down to the flatland.

D.R. was happy. The sound of hysterical yells was so violent that from the reference room we got a call with the advice to behave ourselves, asking us whether we were scientists or small children, and Alex answered that we were stones.

★

That was how we restarted our endless discussions, in midsummer, when nobody was there to disturb us. We had plenty of time to split hairs, to chat, and to wonder what we were going to put in that report for The Science Foundation, whose support depends upon the critical judgements of critical expert reviewers, their appraisal of our probability of success, and their evaluation of our capability to make contributions.

In this century, there is hardly an educated layman who has doubts about the fertility of science, but very few to enjoy the tension between what appears to be true and what is true, between what is pretended and what is real. This tension was an appeal to our minds to see beneath the surface appearance, and to recognize the contradiction between what scientists say they are and what they are.

God knows how hard we tried to smooth our communication with colleagues, peers, all the bloody scientific community, and, of course, the Science Foundation, to which we had to submit a good report a very good one, in order to satisfy the supercritical judgement of supercritical reviewers.

As teachers, we had always a thorough grasp of the subject. We were always in control, keeping our wits and never losing patience and sight of the principal points; plucking from the mass of ideas what is important. This time, we had only one hundred and twenty eight pages at our disposal, and the sentences had to be brief and to the point. Its purpose was to explain how to build a knowledge-based system, and not about our illusion that there is no knowledge at all when looking at the world from outside through vague concepts, which converge into a point of maximal vagueness.

We knew that real knowledge can be obtained only by interaction with the cause of the world, but we had no idea how this task could be achieved by machines. This was our problem that summer. D.R. thought we meant it in a figurative sense, that we were joking as we had often in the past. Dan answered that we really did not have any idea, and he managed to postpone a conclusion. D.R. was categorical, wondering how we were going to convince the Science Foundation.

This was our problem that summer, and the truth is, this was our problem for a long time, if not from the very beginning. It started from the moment we got the key to that historical room in the old department of physics, and Dan brought his electrical boiler to boil his herb tea, and Alex discovered the reference room, and Andrew started to read the poetry of Cavafi, and John discovered John Philiponus who opened the imperial eyes about the fallacy of aristotelian thinking.

Dan was the first to try to see what could be done. He took her with him to play tennis. There, she was visible, with muscles in permanent action. Her gorgeous legs were perfectly tanned, yellowish brown. Some people tan quickly. Dan always liked the brown color of sunburnt skin, but her skin was silk. D.R. had said that she is the goddess of beauty and Dan quickly agreed.

But D.R., being less sober than Dan, didn't keep secret this finding, and told her about the sweet tang of brown skins. She laughed as if she were the goddess of joy. Her laugh was so healthy, coming from her entire body and soul, that very soon we could not imagine our lives without it.

We went out together. Her laughter, loud in cascades, was considered either heavenly trumpets by Dan, or elements of an imperial symphony by Alex and Andrew. But we never knew what was in her mind, because the cascades were the same all the time. We were too intellectual; too proud to make false steps.

A sign that something was in the offing came when Dan seemed to be hurt, and told us that the cascades of laughter produced by the goddess of beauty and joy were disturbing the papers on his desk. D.R. replied, "No, you have to be kidding." Andrew said "Nonsense, you are exhausted. Take a vacation."

Dan went skiing for two weeks. Upon his return he found the angel laughing more loud than ever. Andrew asked him to try to adapt to it. But we still did not know what was in her mind because the cascades were the same. D.R. was too intellectual, and Andrew too proud to make false steps. It seems nothing is more fragile than a young Ph.D.

The second sign that something was in the offing was when D.R. seemed to be hurt, and told us that there are limits for everything, and that he could not work because of her noise. Dan responded, "No, you have to be kidding." Andrew said "Nonsense, you are exhausted, take a vacation." D.R. went skiing for two weeks, and when he came back the girl was laughing louder than before.

Since that time, they didn't get along well. Dan used to say that D.R. is sort of superficial. D.R. used to say that Dan is out of the question.

One day D.R. came up with the idea that mind is nothing else than the behavior of the brain. Skeptical, Dan answered him that today, cognition is considered to be a high-level process. It cannot be understood in the terms of firing of individual neurons, anymore than a computer program can be understood in terms of the bits flitting through an individual register.

D.R. didn't give up and came up with examples. He told us that in 1925, the German neurologist Vogt found, reported the Journal of the American Medical Association, that the genius of Lenin can be explained by the large number of paths proceeding form the pyramidal cells in the cerebral cortex. They were supposed to explain the wide range and the multiplicity of ideas that developed in his brain, and particularly his capacity for quickly getting his bearings when confronted with the most complex situations and problems.

The girl's cascades of laughter were unbelievable, and we all laughed out of control; even Dan laughed.

Then Andrew lost his position as the favorite tennis partner of the goddess of joy. That happened when he talked about a continuous consciousness which cannot be reduced to the discreteness of language. The girl answered him that this was the old story of the overbaked pantheism which says that the goal of meditation is the leaving of the logically structured consciousness in order to attempt an interaction with a God who is inside the world. Old stories. For her God was a person, linked to her by Its Word, in a relationship which opened the door for the knowledge of the rationale of all things.

D.R. responded by saying that we can unlock the unconscious. That there is new evidence of Freud's inner world, and that the workings of this unconscious may be more extensive and sophisticated that even Freud dreamed. He was predicting a grand alliance of psychoanalysis, cognitive psychology, and the biological study of the brain.

John Philiponus said that there is more to it than that. The girl played tennis more and more with John, talking for hours, God knows about what. Later, the news leaked out.

For him, everything started when he asked what death was and formulated some additional questions. The answers were that we are mortals, in the realm of time; outside time only the sacred exists. It took him a long time to understand this last word, until in his sixteenth year of life, when some rod-shaped bacilli infested his lungs, and he felt the danger of being secluded; separated from the healthy crowd outside.

At that moment, he knelt down and had his first serious discussion with God. He bargained and said, "Look, give me a hand. In return, I will be one of your stones."

By pure chance, a fungus very hostile to his tiny bacilli was immediately discovered in England, and so he recovered and went to school.

There he noticed that there are different views. Some colleagues were convinced that God is pure spirit, eternal creator and absolute master of things. Others were sure that God has a Son, while those who were skeptical systematically avoided the topic.

Then, some of his teachers told him that God is fiction, and reality only matter in permanent change, a change which was not expected to change. Puzzled, he wanted to understand. The answer was to orient himself toward science, which minutely describes facts, objects, and phenomena; and tries to link them by what we call laws. If you understand all these laws, you will be able to predict events in the future. You may rest assured that scientific descriptions will replace the amazement of ignorance by the sureness of knowledge.

He did not know what would become of our lives without science. He even tried to observe a law experimentally by looking at effects and causes. He investigated his friends, asking them if they felt God. They said yes, and he said that this had to be a statistical law.

He heard about views from Abott's whimsical tale *Flatland*, a romance of many dimensions which takes place in a flat world populated by lines, circles, and squares. On one occasion, Abott's hero, a square, is visited by a three-dimensional sphere who lifts the flatlander so that he can see the wonders of highness. The square discovers that his planar world is merely a section of another dimensional world.

John did not jump to imagine a four-dimensional world. He did not reason that just as the shadow cast by a three-dimensional object is two-dimensional, so, by analogy, the shadow cast by a four-dimensional object would be three-dimensional. No. He did not jump, because he was not that jumpy. But he liked the idea of scale, promoted by his professor of physics with the example of the gray powder. If one mixes white flour with soot, and an insect of the size of the grains moves around in this powder, for it, there will be no gray powder, but only black and white boulders. On its scale, the view of gray powder does not exist. Only God's view is a good view, because He does not aggregate partial views. Be like Him and you will have the same view.

It was, probably, for that reason that he considered the possiblity of a direct confrontation with what was called direct knowledge.

The small abbey was almost forgotten, hidden up in the mountains, known only by the shepherds. Behind old walls covered with climbing white flowers was a small chapel, as a boat in a natural harbor. Protected by flowers, the old monk was supposed to restore the original Garden of Eden.

When John entered his cell, he saw only a bed and an icon. The whole place was filled with the noise of bees, the rays of the sun and with peace, all spread over the white of the cell, and over the icon, a painting that deliberately neglected depth perspective. The scene proved that what is human is important in so far as what is divine shines through it.

John spent a week there. He wanted to know what these men are doing who want to identify themselves with the cause of the world, which they believe, is God's thinking. The monk never used such categories as time, space, object, number, and causality. He perceived the world as an undifferentiated whole from which he was not distinct. In the stillness of his prayer, he was looking over space, at some undefined point.

Nobody knows exactly what happened. John finished college, bought his first car, had his first crash, and for a while, walked with a plaster cast. Everybody called him the man with the foot bare. Then he met a beautiful angel, got married, and kept an eye on what was happening at the abbey. The beautiful angel painfully tried to commit herself to only one person, later turned into a bundle of raw emotions, and finally finished by finding a different view in each man she met, restlessly searching for one who had the most views.

He felt the danger, knelt down and had another discussion with Him. He said "Look, give me a chance, I cannot afford to be a big stone. So how about my being a small one?"

Whoever does not ascend, falls, for by remaining with one partial view for a long time, gazing at one aspect only, a man grows dull.

It was love at first whirl, which was what Alex said, and what Andrew said, and what Dan said. When we met, we knew that this is a miracle. At least this is what we heard from Alex, notorious as a compulsive scholar; from Dan, who in no time at all had become addicted to elocution; and from Andrew, who was so fond of claiming that he is a musician. Even from D.R., who like many other floundering apostates before him sought to steady himself with the wisdom of the old patriarchs, admitted to this.

We all were very young, looking for a conductor to convey the composer's ideas: to follow the score, to wave the baton with grace, to keep an eye on the singers, to make a sign to the drums, to the Dutch horn, and so on. Together, we had had the unbelievable, unthinkable, unspeakable hope of understanding the mind. John believed that our mind is an exodus, like the exodus from Egypt; a type of conversion from the fall into pieces, back to the primordial condition. It was not an abandonment of a present condition for the sake of a condition that is totally new, but a return to a normality which has been lost. It constituted an advance of spiritual nature, which occurs in a kind of abyss perceived only when the familiar forms of knowing are recognized as masks or views hiding a deeper reality.

When we started our discussions, we knew only that anything which opposes the pullback towards the original point represents evil. Once in possession of this simple idea, we thought that by torturing it and treating it like a plastic, we would succeed in molding it into distinct shapes, fit to explain a number of facts.

The idea of focusing our attention on the nonaristotelian logic started with John's obsession about a God that is unknown and known. He tried something not tried before. He used positive and negative predicates simultaneously, convinced that in this way, the standards of reference won't be revised by new observations.

This speculation scared Andrew, who was too young, too shy, and too cautious from the beginning. He married my love, the capricorn woman, and moved to New York.

We met Andrew after one year in Fort Tyron Park, at the Cloisters, a branch of the Metropolitan Museum of Art. It was a modern structure with parts of medieval buildings from Spain and France.

He told us that during the period of divorce, his wife was obsessed by an adagio by Albinoni. We asked him what happened. Tom Albinoni, he answered, has to be remembered because Bach had used some of his works. He had based four fugues on subjects by the Venetian musician.

We asked him where is she now. He answered that the listener is rarely aware of his compositional virtuosity but is invariably bewitched by the work's mesmerizing beauty.

"The rich and expressive art of Venice," we continued. "We were on the beach," answered Andrew. Every man stopped dead in his tracks, hearts skipped a beat waves stalled in midair. She was a seraph of splendor. She left. Period.

We admired together the carvings of elaborate figurative motifs, the painted wood ceilings, the stain glass, and the rich tapestries depicting unicorns and big flowering gardens. He recognized rosemary, jasmine, citrus, aloe, bay, and possibly acanthus. We recognized narcissus, grape, hyacinth, and crocus; concrete examples of matter in its original beauty. Together, we decided that man has a power to redeem creation through art.

This last observation caused a great deal of comment. Finally, we agreed that if flesh became a vehicle of the spirit, then so, though in a different way, so can wood, paint, and icons.

We stopped in front of a tapestry representing the unicorn in captivity. "Woven threads," remarked Andrew, "like our report to the Science Foundation. A picture written by monks."

We agreed. It is not so much what monks do that matters, but what they are. When they call thousands of times without interruption upon His name, in the rhythm of the breath, saying, "Lord have mercy upon me, the sinner," then the heart swallows up God and God swallows the heart. No doubt about that, the contemplative is penetrated by light, like the one on Mount Tabor.

Andrew asked us about our work, our grant, and our relationship with the Science Foundation. We told him that everything was quite alright, and that even D.R. has changed. The dapper, undisputed king of the campus has shocked, saddened, and some say, given a certain amount of perverse satisfaction to many.

Andrew asked for more details.

We told him that D.R. now says that a thirteen hundred year old man, Petrus Sabatius Stirbey, speaks words of wisdom through him. His new message was that the Valley of Danube will be the safest place in a future filled with all kinds of pollution. For instance bigotry, where there is a temptation of confusing the Spirit of God with the spirit of one party; or intolerance, which comes with the temptation of confusing the Spirit of God with the spirit of man.

Outside, in the park, we heard the blurred sound of children, joyfully playing with their mothers. An undifferentiated whole from which we were not distinct.

We asked Andrew if he wants to come back. The seminar was still running. With a wistful longing for something he had known in the past, Andrew said yes. For him, it was a cool breeze in that hot summer. What else could be better? He seemed to look wistfully at the image of himself, laughing.

Then, we switched to the report. We had been postponing it for another full year. You know D.R. and his connections. The existing draft had to be revised, and new sources had to be developed. "The report has to be a guide for the perplexed," we added. "Like the tapestry of the unicorn," he added. "Presenting things one has not noticed previously. And, therefore, uncharted expanses of the universe," we added, "Openings revealed to us with sometimes painful clarity," he added.

Andrew asked for more details about D.R. We told him we had sent a new paper to be published. D.R. wrote an excellent review, saying that our contribution is a fresh synthesis rooted in the real nonaristotelian tradition, beautifully open to the legitimate concerns of what we call contemporary science. Much more he wrote for us as the nonaristotelian logic gradually discovers its mission and formulates its message, it is important that its roots be solidly planted. No doubt about that: there cannot be science without continuity, consistency, and an awareness of unity with those who are practicing science in different circumstances.

Andrew said that the new text of the report had to be complete, based on unquestionable documents and on first-hand knowledge; a written account of our experience: a memoir. This approach would avoid intellectual dilution; it will effectively raise, rather than lower, the level of presentation.

He gave us an example. Sullivan's *Heirs of the Roman Empire*, a narrative essay on the history of our tradition, from its origins to the present.

Not interested in our discussion, the unicorn was gazing over space, at an undefined point. His strange behavior caused a good deal of comments. First, it was clear that though it would fight savagely when cornered, it could be tamed by a virgin's touch. Second, it had a horn.

Andrew remembered Daniel's dream from the reference room. We told him that the girl piled up new evidence to prove that 1944 was a good approximation for the beginning of the end of the world, when the goats will be separated from the sheep.

"The capricorn is a goat," murmured Andrew.

Our sudden and violent burst of laughter shocked the unicorn, the guards in the gallery and two pigeons who happened to be on the window.

We restarted our discussions in June, on the longest day of the year, when the campus was empty.